A pictorial Chronicle of Siena

William Heywood

BIBLIOLIFE

A
PICTORIAL CHRONICLE
OF SIENA

BY

WILLIAM HEYWOOD

AUTHOR OF

Our Lady of August and the Palio of Siena ;
The "Ensamples" of Fra Filippo, a study
of Mediæval Siena, &c.

.... Many coloured tablets bright
With loves and wars of old.
Lord MACAULAY.

SIENA,
ENRICO TORRINI, PUBLISHER.

—

1902.
All rights reserved.

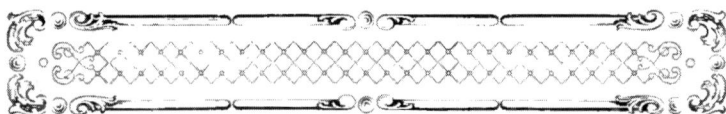

PREFACE.

There are, of course, at least two ways of
looking at old pictures. We may seek only for
" artistic pleasure", judging them entirely according to their possession or lack of the five elements
of decoration: 1) significance of form, 2) pattern,
3) colour, 4) space-composition, and 5) richness
of material and texture; or, starting with the
axiom that " the proper study of mankind is
man," we may prefer to regard them simply as
literature, endeavouring to see with the eyes of the
men who painted them, and to learn what life
was like in the days when the refulgence of their

the coronations of Popes and Emperors. Not unfrequently, indeed, where they are devoid of artistic merit, I have unhesitatingly relegated Tavolette of the latter class to the list at the end of the volume.

It only remains to add that I am indebted in a very special manner to the learned works of Signor Cav. Alessandro Lisini and Prof. Paoli, with which I have headed my list of authorities.

WILLIAM HEYWOOD.

Siena, *Villa Ventena*, April 1902.

TABLE OF CONTENTS.

———

List of Illustrations. .. ..Page   11

Principal Authorities   13

The Offices of Biccherna and of Gabella   15

The painted book-covers of Biccherna and of Gabella.   37

     I... The Tavolette of the XIIIth and XIVth
Centuries   37

     II.. The Tavolette of the XVth Century.   50

     III. The Tavolette of the XVIth Century   81

List of the Tavolette..   105

Chronological Table of the Principal Sienese Painters   117

Index   121

———

LIST OF ILLUSTRATIONS.

PLATE I. The Coronation of Our Lady by Sano
di Pietro .. .. Frontispiece

» II. Photograph of Entry in the *Libro di Biccherna* of 13 July 1282 .. .. .. Page 22

» III. Coats of Arms of the Provveditori. *Tavoletta di Biccherna* of 1263. 33

» IV. Don Ugo Camarlingo del Comune. *Tavoletta di Biccherna* of 1258. 38

» V. *Tavoletta di Biccherna* of 1314.. 50

» VI. The Madonna recommending the City
of Siena to her Divine Son. *Tavoletta di Gabella* of 1480 74

» VII. Marriage of Lucrezia Malavolti. *Tavoletta di Gabella* of 1473 80

» VIII. Allegorical Picture. *Tavoletta di Gabella*
of 1542.. 88

PRINCIPAL AUTHORITIES.

A. LISINI, *Le Tavolette dipinte di Biccherna e di Gabella del R. Archivio di Stato in Siena.* (This book, which has been more recently printed than any of the other works here cited, bears neither date nor name of publisher. It is a volume of about 14 inches in height, 10$\frac{1}{2}$ in depth and 2$\frac{1}{2}$ in breadth. It contains excellent reproductions of all the Tavolette together with an introduction and commentary.)

C. PAOLI, *Le Tavolette dipinte della Biccherna e della Gabella nell'Archivio di Stato di Siena.* Discorso accademico del dì 23 agosto 1891 (Siena, Tip. Ancora, 1891).

L. MUSSINI, *Le Tavole della Biccherna e della Gabella della Repubblica di Siena.* Lettura (Adunanza del dì 17 luglio 1877). — In *"Atti e Memorie della Sezione letteraria e di storia patria della R. Accademia dei Rozzi di Siena."* Nuova Serie, vol. III, p. 27. — Cfr. *Rassegna Settimanale di Roma*, II, 270-272, fasc. del 20 ottobre 1878. — The same

article was published in French in the periodical *L'Art*, 1877, to. IX, pp. 225-232, under the title *Les Couvertures des livres de Biccherna et de Gabella de la République de Sienne.*

A. GEFFROY, *Tablettes inédites de la Biccherna et de la Gabella de Sienne*, in "*Mélanges d'Archéologie et d'Histoire publiés par l'École française de Rome*," 1882, to. II, pp. 415-434.

L. BANCHI, *Copertura di un libro sanese del 1498* in *Il Bibliofilo*, anno I, marzo 1880, pp. 33-35.

F. ELLON, *Tavolette dipinte della Biccherna di Siena che si conservano nel Museo di Berlino*, in "*Bullettino Senese di Storia Patria*," vol. II (1895), pp. 101-110.

La Sala della Mostra e il Museo delle Tavolette dipinte della Biccherna e della Gabella nel R. Archivio di Stato in Siena, omaggio al IV Congresso storico italiano (Siena, Lazzeri, 1889).

G. B. CAVALCASELLE and J. A. CROWE, *A New History of Painting in Italy* (London, John Murray, 1864), vol. I, p. 179.

B. BERENSON, *The Central Italian Painters of the Renaissance* (London & New York, G. P. Putnam's sons, 1897). Index to the works of the principal Central Italian Painters, pp. 131 et seq.

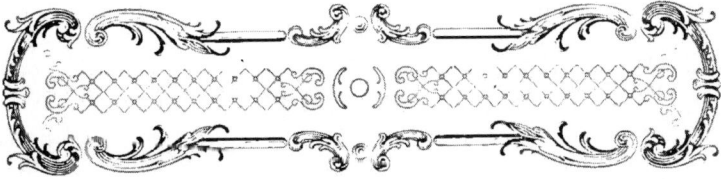

THERE are in Siena two of the most curious specimens of artistic paleography which the world has ever seen. One is the celebrated Cathedral Pavement, the other the Covers of the old Treasury Registers of the Republic, better known by their Italian title of the *Tavolette dipinte della Biccherna e della Gabella*. Of these the latter is unquestionably the most worthy of study, not only because the *Tavolette* do not labour under the disadvantages of position and material which detract so fatally from the merits of the Pavement regarded as a series of pictographs, although as a whole it is no doubt sufficiently imposing,[1] but also because,

---

[1] " It is a work in which the talents of the Artist and the materials employed are alike perverted to the least appropriate uses ; but it is much admired by persons who like to be amused with the ingenious artifices of misapplied skill."—C. E. NORTON, *Historical studies of Church Building in the Middle Ages* (New York, Harper & Bros., 1880), page 176 note.

entirely apart from their enormous value as works
of art, they possess an historical importance which
it would be hard to overestimate, constituting,
in fact, a pictorial chronicle of the Mediæval
Commune.

The *Tavolette dipinte* being, as I have said,
book-covers, it will be convenient to commence
our enquiry with a brief account of the two great
administrative offices of Biccherna and of Gabella
to which the books in question belonged.

In Siena, from the earliest times, a large part
of the business of the government was transacted
by *Balìe* or Commissions of *Boni homines*. Indeed, according to Professor Zdekauer,[1] the *Balìa*
was " the original and primitive form in which
the political life of the Commune manifested itself ",
all the magistracies, nay even the Legislative
Council itself, the *Consiglio Generale della Campana,* being in their inception nothing more than
provisionary commissions which in process of time
became permanent. If this theory be correct, it
would be impossible to discover a better example
of the development of a *Balìa* into a permanent
and powerful magistracy acting upon its own responsibility than is afforded us by the *Biccherna,*
which, coeval in its origin with the first days of

---

[1] L. ZDEKAUER, *La vita pubblica dei Senesi nel Dugento* (Siena,
Lazzeri, 1897), pages 12, 13. See also the *Dissertation* which precedes
the same author's magnificent edition of *Il Constituto del Comune di
Siena dell'anno 1262* (Milano, U. Hoepli, 1897 , page XXII.

civic liberty, continued to exist for more than six centuries and long outlived the Commune which gave it birth. Of the *Provveditori (provisores, proveditores)*, as the officials who presided in Biccherna were called, we have record as early as 1167, nineteen years before the Republic was formally recognised in the name of the Empire by Henry VI.; while the magistracy in question was only finally abolished by Pietro Leopoldo in 1786.

The etymology of the word *Biccherna* has given rise to almost as much discussion as that of our *Exchequer*. According to most writers it is derived from the German *bücker* (book): but Signor Lisini is disposed to think that it is more likely that the magistracy took its name from the place where it originally sat. At the end of the XIIth century the Consuls held their sessions in a building which belonged to the parish church of San Pellegrino and which was called *Bacherna* or *Bicherna*. Here too were to be found the Provveditori who, with their *Camarlingo (Camerarius)*, administered the public revenues; as also, at a later period, the Court of the Potestà and the offices of sundry minor functionaries. In the year 1275 the Provveditori were left alone *in Biccherna*, all the rest of the officials having removed elsewhere; and it is therefore probable that they acquired their name from this circumstance.[1]

---

[1] A. LISINI, *Le Tavolette dipinte*, &c., pages III-IV. — That the officials of Biccherna remained in San Pellegrino until the Palazzo Pubblico was erected in the Piazza del Campo is proved by the entries in

From the first this magistracy seems to have consisted of a Chancellor or *Camarlingo* and four Provveditori, a number which was scarcely ever increased or diminished. It is true that for a brief period, towards the middle of the thirteenth century, there were only three Provveditori, while, after the popular victory of 1371, the desire of extending the honours and emoluments of government to as many of the *Popolari* as possible led to the nomination of sometimes six and sometimes seven officials; but even then, although their number was well nigh doubled, they still bore their old title of the *Quattro Provveditori*.

At first the office of Camarlingo was occupied by a citizen; but afterwards, for many years and especially between 1275 and 1349, it was, as a rule, conferred upon a member of the monastic orders, generally a Cistercian of San Galgano or one of the Frati Umiliati. Nor can we greatly wonder at such a choice when we remember that both these orders lived under the rule of St. Benedict and consequently numbered among their members many men of ability and learning. The monastery of San Galgano in particular had acquired such consideration and importance that its monks were often called to arbitrate upon the most difficult and delicate questions;[1] while in

---

their books regarding the rent paid by them, e. g. that of December 1282: *Item xv lib. domino Gregorio de Sancto Peregrino pro pensione Biccherne, primiis vj mensibus* (Libri di Biccherna, ad annum, c. 127).

[1] Thus, for example, in 1215 the Abbot of San Galgano acted

its cloisters were to be found not only theologians and canonists, jurists, notaries and physicians, but also artificers and architects.[1]

Later on preference seems to have been once more given to laymen, but their integrity was not always above suspicion and friars were still occasionally selected. In 1427 Fra Bernardino, while preaching in the Piazza del Campo, vehemently denounced the burdening of " the religious " with secular duties;[2] and so great was his influence that for nearly a quarter of a century no friar or monk was made Camarlingo. In 1452

as arbitrator in a dispute between the Commune of Siena and Pagano Pannocchieschi Bishop of Volterra concerning the rights which the former possessed in the Castello di Montieri—ARCH. DI STATO IN SIENA, Caleffo dell'Assunta, c. 9t, 10 – while in 1218 the Abbot of San Galgano was commissioned by Pope Honorius III. to ascertain whether certain accusations made against the Bishop of Fiesole were well founded—UGHELLI, Italia Sacra, tom. III, col. 321.

1 Compare A. CANESTRELLI, L'Abbazia di San Galgano (Firenze, Fratelli Alinari, 1896), pages 15 et seq.

2 Le prediche volgari di San Bernardino da Siena, dette nella Piazza del Campo, l'anno MCCCCXXVII, ora primamente edite da L. BANCHI (Siena, tip. S. Bernardino, 1880), vol. III, 217-218. — "Non si die impacciare il religioso a le cose seculari, no. Doh, ditemi cittadini : voi fate i vostri bossoli : mettetevi voi e' frati ? Se voi ve gli mettete, mettetevi anco me. Voi vi date a crédare che i vostri camarlenghi del Comuno secolari abbino furato di quello del Comuno, e però forse gli volete fare che sieno frati. E' frati forse non furano ? Oh, egli è il mal segno, che per questo voi vogliate camarlengo religioso ! O che benedizione è questa, che voi aviate sospetto l'uno dell' altro ? Io ve l' ho detto e dico per detto di Pavolo : non v' impacciate de' religiosi. Non basta egli che voi andiate a casa del diavolo per volere i vostri uffizî, senza che voi v' ingegnate di cacciarvi anco noi ? "

That from a very early period complaints regarding the general corruption of the officials were frequent, see L. ZDEKAUER, La vita pubblica, &c., op. cit., page 14 note.

there was a reversion to the old system, but it only continued for seven years after which the office was filled exclusively by laymen.

The Camarlingo and the Quattro Provveditori were elected every six months, their terms of office running from the first of January to the thirtieth of June, and from the first of July to the thirty-first of December.

It is no easy matter to give even a faint idea of the importance of the Magistracy of Biccherna in the early days of the Commune when, by reason of the multiplicity and scope of its administrative functions, it must have formed a considerable factor in the daily life of almost every member of a wealthy and enterprising community. Into the Biccherna were poured the customs, the *prestanze*, the fines, the taxes levied for concessions of privileges and monopolies, and whatever other assessments, imposts or tributes went to make up the revenues of the State. Thither came the officials of the Republic, the professors of the University, the ambassadors and the commissaries to draw their salaries; there the heads of the guilds, the artisans and the mechanics who were engaged upon the public works, the painters and architects in the employ of the Commune, received their wages; there alms were distributed monthly to mendicant friars and to the poor; while there also the *berrovieri* of the Potestà, the ministers of justice and the mercenary troops who were hired by the government were paid for their services.

In fact, in the office of Biccherna, on every day of the year, except the festivals of Holy Church, a perpetual stream of persons of all ranks and ages was passing to and fro from morning till night, intent either to receive or to pay money in larger or smaller sums.

Thus the Books of Biccherna contain entries of the most interesting and varied character; such, for example, as the amount expended for perches for the falcons wherewith the Emperor Frederick II. went a hawking in the plains of Orgia; [1] the price of the purple mantle which the ill-starred Corradino offered on the altar of Our Lady of Grace before he set forth to meet his doom at the hands of Charles of Anjou; [2] and, two years later, the sums paid to Ventura, the painter, for emblazoning the arms of that same Charles upon

---

[1] April 1247: *Item xxxiiij sol., et iij den. Bonico Bonici castaldo Comunis quos solvit pro perfacimento lignorum que habuit et operatus est pro facendis lecteriis domini Imperatoris et pro stanchis pro ponendis falconibus eidem domini Imperatoris apud episcopatum, cum venit Senis.—Item v. sol. domino Bernardino Johannis Pape pro sua ambasciata cum uno equo quando ivit in planum Orgie et ad partes illas providenda roveria pro domino Imperatore, qui volebat ire venatum*—vol. XIV, c. 12*l.*

[2] June 1268: *Item xiiij lib., xvij sol., quos dictus Camerarius solvit in presentia dictorum Quatuor, Arringerio zendadario et sotiis, de quibus fuerunt novem libre pro quadam purpura quam oblavit dominus Rex Curadus in suo aventu in altare sancte Marie, et quinque libre et decem et septem sol. fuerunt pro tribus pennonibus pro capiendo et ponendo campo et una bandiera* (c. 103).

There are numerous entries in the *Libri di Biccherna* touching the expenses incurred to do honour to Corradino. Of these the most important have been collected by Dott. A. PROFESSIONE in his *Corradino di Svevia e il suo passaggio per Siena*, and by A. LISINI, *op. cit.*, pages V-VI, notes.

the *Carroccio* of the imperial city,[1] and to messer
Deo Tolomei and the other Guelfs for destroying the tower and palace of Provenzano Salvani.[2]
Elsewhere are entered the wages earned by the
officers of justice who burned the false-coiner Capocchio ;[3] the fines paid by Cecco Angiolieri and
by the Florentine Casella, him whom Dante

> woo'd to sing
> Met in the milder shades of Purgatory,

both of them condemned for wandering about
the streets at night after the ringing of the Curfew ;[4] the sums given as compensation to citizens

---

[1] *Item xt sol. den. quos dictus Camerarius solvit Venture, pic-*
tori qui pinxit arma regis Caruli in carroccio (vol. XXXVIII, 1270,
ind. XIII, da Sett. a Feb., c. 90).

[2] *Item l lib. quas* [Camerarius] *dedit et solvit Guelchis, qui dis-*
sipaverunt turrim filiorum Salvani — Item lxxxxiiij libr. quas dedit
et solvit domino Deo de Tolomeis pro dissipando palatium filiorum
Salvani — Item x lib. Iacobo Albertini pro faciendo sgombrare stra-
tam apud Sanctum Cristoforum de lapidibus domus Provenzanorum
et cet. (vol. XL, 1270, c. 9, 10, 11).

[3] *Item xxxviiij sol. dicta die* (5 August 1293) *in uno fiorino de*
auro, tribus Ribaldis qui fecerunt unam giustitiam, ideo quod fece-
runt comburi CAPOCCHIUM *et interfecerunt filium Ser Guidi de Po-*
mecta (vol. LXVIII, c. 121).

[4] Casella appears to have been twice condemned for the same
offence, on the 13th and 21st July 1282, the first time in company
with Cecco Angiolieri, the second alone.

Item xx sol. die dicta a CECCHO *domini Angiulieri Sulaficha,*
quia fuit invenctus de nocte, post tertium sonum Campane Comunis,
que pulsatur de sero.

Item xx sol., xiij Iulii a CASELLA, *homine Curie, quia fuit in-*
ventus de nocte post tertium sonum Campane Comunis.

Item xx sol., die dicta a SCARSELLA *de Florentia, homine Curie,*
quia fuit inventus de nocte post tertium sonum Campane Comunis
(c. 1, 2).

PLATE II.

whose houses had been destroyed or damaged by
fire;[1] the price of garments bestowed in charity
upon an indigent feudal seignior whom the new
order of things had reduced to beggary;[2] the fee
paid to a notary for rewriting a portion of the
statutes which had been torn to pieces by a pet
monkey of the Potestà;[3] the cost of the paper
and parchment used in the public offices,[4] and
the money expended for ornamenting the covers
of their books;[5] in a word, innumerable entries

---

[1] *Infrascripti sunt denarii quos solvimus illis personis quibus
fuerunt dissipate domus occasione ignis . . . . et solvimus eis secundum
formam statuti* (vol. XCI, c. 314).

See L. ZDEKAUER, *La vita privata dei Senesi nel Dugento* (Siena,
Lazzeri, 1896), pages 35-36, and compare C. FALLETTI-FOSSATI, *Costumi senesi nella seconda metà del secolo XIV*, page 98.

[2] *Item iij lib. in una tunicha, quam habuit Nicholaus, comes de
Roccha ad Telenanum, causa paupertatis : et est habita inde appodissa a dominis novem* (1296, c. 233, Usc.) - *Item, iij lib. xi sol. vj
den. in quadam tunica et in uno caputio et uno pario chaligarum
datis pro amore dei Niccholaio de Tintinnano* (1298, c. 202t).

[3] *Item vj sol. Ser Goro notario quia scripsit unum quaternum
Constituti Palatii quos* (sic) *delaniaverat simmia domini Comitis*
(1887, da Gennaio, c. 49).

[4] See the *Miscellanea storica senese*, vol. V (1898), pages 57-59.

[5] 1258. *Item v sol., Gilio pictori, pro miniis que fecit in libro Camerarii et dictorum trium, parabola et presentia predictorum* (c. 3t).

1263. *Item x sol. Barbarino custodi Biccherne ut eos daret Magistro qui pinxit libros Camerarii et quatuor* (c. 80t).

1264. *Item x sol. Dietisalvi depignitori pro pictura librorum Camerarii et iiij quos solvit dictus Camerarius parabola iiij.or* (c. 29).

1267. *Item xl sol., quos solvit Dietisalvi pictori, eo quod pinxit
duos libros Camerarii et iiij et unum vesillum Terzerii Sancti Martini* (c. 230).

1280. *Item x sol. Guidoni pictori, pro pictura librorum Camerarii
et quattuor* (c. 17).

1282. *Item viij sol. die xxiiij Iulii Dietisalvi pictori quia depinsit* (sic) *librum Camerarii et iiij in quibus scripte sunt earum intrate
et expense* (c. 84t).

of the most miscellaneous and incongruous character, but which in their entirety probably afford us a better idea of the habits, the virtues and the vices of the men of that day than all the chronicles and histories which were ever written.

Although the administrative mechanism of the office was by no means complex, it was well calculated to prevent fraud and malversation. Thus while all disbursements were made by the Camarlingo in person, it was necessary that they should be made in the presence and with the consent of at least two of the Provveditori who were held equally responsible with him for any improper expenditure of the public monies, such responsibility, in fact, only ceasing where a special order in writing had been received from the Governatori or the Potestà.

A notary *(notarius camerarii, scrittore di Biccherna)* sat beside the Camarlingo and entered each payment in a book provided for the purpose, specifying by whose order it was made, and noting which of the Provveditori were present.

With regard to the monies received at least equal precautions were taken. The Camarlingo was not permitted to accept any payments directly. These in the first instance were made to the Provveditori whose duty it was to note why and by whom the sums which they thus received were paid, and to take charge of them until the following day. Then, at last, they were transferred to the Camarlingo, who thereupon caused an entry of the money so consigned to him *(re-assegnata)* to be made in the proper book.

When the treasury was empty, it was the duty of the officials to borrow money on the best terms possible, never however paying a higher rate of interest than that which was usual among the merchants and business men of the city. Moreover, before incurring such a debt, it was necessary to obtain the consent of at least three-quarters of the members of the Consiglio Generale della Campana.

For the superintendence of all these operations the Governatori and the Consoli di Mercanzia appointed another official, who was generally selected from the so called *Terziari* or *homines de Penitentia*, a class of persons who occupied a position midway between friars and laymen, and who, at least in public, posed as rigid moralists and warm supporters of charitable works. This official noted in a separate book all the monies received, paid and transferred in the office of Biccherna, whether by the Camarlingo or by the Provveditori; and he was obliged to submit the same to the inspection of the Governatori and of the Consoli di Mercanzia at the end of each month, as well as upon such other occasions as they might request to see it. His regular term of office was six months, but that period might be prolonged or curtailed at the pleasure of the Consoli and Governatori.

Under the Communal system the power of many of the officials was very great; but, on their retirement from office they were at once divested of all authority and were held strictly accountable for all that they had done amiss. Even the foreign Potestà was obliged to remain in Siena for eight days after the expiration of his term, *pro reddenda ratione administrationis mee et gestionis quam feci ego vel socius meus vel aliquis de familia mea,* while his successor was sworn to hear all complaints made against the out-going officials; and, indeed, from the earliest times, it had been customary to appoint commissioners to enquire into the actions of the retiring magistrates.[1]

In the case of the officials of Biccherna this inquisition was made by three " good, sufficient and legal " men, specially nominated to examine item by item the accounts of the preceding half year. For this purpose they were allowed a period of thirty days which, in 1318, was in-

---

[1] L. ZDEKAUER, *La vita pubblica,* op. cit., page 13.—That even in the case of the highest Magistrates of the Republic these enquiries might lead to very serious consequences let the following passage from the Chronicle of NERI DI DONATO (*ad annum* 1355) bear witness: " La lezione prima de' Signori Dodici di Siena essendo usciti d' Uffizio del mese di Maggio e di Giugno fe' molte e grandi baratterie nel loro Uffizio. Unde el Podestà di Siena fe' inquisizione e processi contra di loro; e prese Misser Giovanni dell'Acqua, el quale era stato de' detti Signori: e trovato el vero, colla mitara in capo per falsario li fe' tagliare la testa; e diede bando a Guccio Pieri, e a Ser Jacomo di Domenico Ricci, che furo insieme de' Signori: non li potè pigliare, però li diede el bando. "

creased to two months. If they discovered any instances of fraudulent or wasteful expenditure, it was their duty to cancel the objectionable items and to charge them to the officials who were responsible for the same. Finally they reported the result of their revision to the Consiglio Generale which thereupon voted the approval or rejection of the accounts in question.

In addition to the receipt and disbursement of public monies, the Camarlingo and the Provveditori were entrusted with innumerable other duties of an extremely heterogeneous character. They nominated the custodians of the public fountains, the *banditori* of the Commune, the *castellani* and other minor officials, either on their own authority or, in certain cases, in conjunction with other magistrates. They supervised the repair and maintenance of the streets, the bridges and the fountains ; they provided for the construction of public buildings, and especially for the excavation of those *bottini* or subterranean waterways which still spread like a network beneath the city. The Provveditori who assumed office in the month of July were further charged to inspect the state armories, to examine the condition of the tents, cross-bows and other implements of warfare, causing the magazine in which they were stored to be opened at least twice a week, to the end that they might be found fit for use at a moment's notice ; while, together with

the Potestà, it was their care to cause the black
and white marble, the bricks and lime, with which
the Republic annually provided the Operaio del
Duomo for the work on the Cathedral, to be
brought from the quarries and kilns of the contado—a labour best performed during the summer
months when the roads were hard and dry.

In process of time the old systems of collecting revenues and tributes were greatly modified;
and, as the methods of administration became
more complicated, the number of chests destined
to contain the public monies increased, until almost every office had one of its own. Thus a
large part of the business formerly transacted in
Biccherna was transferred elsewhere and the Provveditori lost much of that authority and consideration which they had once enjoyed. When Cosimo de' Medici became seignior of Siena, in 1557,
their already sadly diminished powers were still
further curtailed, and, long before the final suppression of their office in the last quarter of the
eighteenth century, they had dwindled into mere
ædiles, one of whose principal remaining duties was
to make arrangements for the running of the Palio.

With regard to the office of *Gabella* a very
few words will suffice.

In the early years of the Commune there was
very little direct taxation, except in the case of
war or other extraordinary emergency. In those
days the penalty of almost every crime might be

commuted for a money payment,[1] while many offences were punished by confiscation of goods. Moreover the large revenues which accrued from these sources were effectually supplemented by a quantity of tolls and customs the ingenuity and number of which might well arouse a feeling of envy in the minds of the acutest modern financiers. The year 1198, however, saw the introduction of the *Lira* or *Estimo,* a system of taxation which was based upon the principle of assessment and which was gradually extended to all the subjects of the Republic until, by the end of the following century, it had become the ordinary means of raising money.[2] About the same time (1290), in order to simplify the work of the administrative officials and to reduce the expense of collecting the public revenues, the plan was adopted of farming out certain dues and imposts; and the management of these transactions was entrusted

---

[1] Compare, for example, §§ 198, 201, 204, 205, 209, 211, 221, 222, 226, &c. of the fifth Distinction of *Il Frammento degli ultimi due libri del più antico Constituto Senese* (1262-1270), published by L. ZDEKAUER, in the *Bullettino senese di storia patria,* vol. III (1896), pages 82 et seq. —The well known story of Anselmo Salimbeni and Angelica Montanini turns upon this practice.—See G. SERMINI, *Novelle* (Livorno, F. Vigo, 1874), page 188.

[2] See L. BANCHI, *La Lira o l'Estimo* in the *Atti della R. Accademia dei Fisiocritici di Siena,* series III, vol. II; also *La Lira, la Tavola delle possessioni e le preste,* by the same author, in the *Arch. stor. it.,* series III, vol. VII, part II (1868), pages 53 et seq.— To those students of Mediæval Italy who are interested in the question of taxation in the XIIIth Century I cannot too strongly recommend Sig. G. SALVEMINI's *Magnati e popolani in Firenze* dal 1280 al 1295 (Firenze, C. Carnesecchi, 1899), chap. II, § 6, pages 50 et seq.

to a new magistracy which was known by the name of the *Ufficio degli Esecutori di Gabella.*

By the Esecutori the right of collecting the dues which were charged at the gates of the city [1] and in the public markets, the taxes imposed upon the vendors of certain comestibles, the tolls paid by those who frequented the baths of the contado,[2] traversed certain roads, or bridges, or rented piazze, shops and houses, were sold to the highest bidders. Even the custody of the gaols was put up to auction;[3] while the public coffers were yet further enriched by the sale of numerous monopolies,[4] not the least among which was the privilege of conducting games of chance such as *tavole* and *zara.*[5] However the principal duty of

---

[1] See the *Statuto della gabella e dei passaggi dalle porte della città di Siena* (1301-1303) published by L. BANCHI among the *Statuti senesi* (Bologna, G. Romagnoli, 1871), vol. II.

[2] For some account of the baths of the Sienese contado see W. HEYWOOD, *The " Ensamples " of Fra Filippo, a study of Mediæval Siena* (Siena, Torrini, 1901), pages 75-80.

[3] In those days, as is well known, the Commune paid absolutely nothing towards the maintenance of its prisoners, and the indigent among them were consequently almost entirely dependent upon the charitable. The keepers of the gaol exacted from each of its inmates the sum of 10 *soldi* if his term of imprisonment lasted for more than two days and 5 *soldi* for a shorter period. Thus a man who was liberated on the same day on which he was incarcerated paid 5 *soldi*. If his imprisonment was for debt, his gaoler was entitled to demand 2 *denari* for every *lira* owed ; and until his dues were paid, he might decline to release his prisoner.

[4] See, for a good example, *L'appalto della gabella della spazzatura in piazza*, published by L. ZDEKAUER, *La vita pubblica*, &c., *op. cit.*, pages 116-117, Appendice VI.

[5] As to the games of chance played by the Sienese in the XIIIth and XIVth centuries, see W. HEYWOOD, *op. cit.*, chapter IV, § 2.

the Esecutori was the collection of the taxes due upon devises, dowries and the sale and purchase of both real and personal property—in a word, on all contracts whether drawn and attested by a notary or not.

Originally the Esecutori della Gabella were three in number (one for each Terzo of the City) and were presided over by a foreign judge (*iudex foretaneus*) and by a monk or friar as Camarlingo. They were elected by the Consiglio Generale, and remained in office for six months. Later on, as was the case with the Provveditori di Biccherna and for the same reasons, their numbers were increased from three to five, and even to six; but, this change proving prejudicial to the dispatch of public business, they were reduced to four in 1399, and the *Quattro Esecutori* they remained until the suppression of their office in 1808 during the French domination of Tuscany.[1]

Both in Biccherna and in Gabella a new set of books was opened with each election of new officials, so that fresh registers were required every six months. Of these there were three, two of which were used in Biccherna and one in Gabella. In the first half of each book were entered the monies received *(Entrata, Introitus)*, in the second half the monies spent *(Uscita, Exitus)*. The

---

[1] For the foregoing account of the Magistracies of the Biccherna and the Gabella I am mainly indebted to Sig. A. LISINI, *op. cit.*, pages III-IX.

most ancient registers of Biccherna were composed of parchment, as also were those of Gabella. These volumes, which measured between
fourteen and fifteen inches in length and from
nine to ten inches in depth, were at first bound
with the utmost simplicity, being merely enclosed
between two wooden boards *(tavole, tavolette)*,
connected only by a leather strap or band, so
that the backs were left uncovered. Thus protected
they were stored away among the archives of the
office to which they belonged. Before long, however, these bare and unornamented boards became an eyesore to the good citizens of Siena,
whose artistic feeling was so early manifested in
the embellishment of their city; and, in the first
half of the XIIIth century, they began to emblazon
upon the Tavolette the arms of the Camarlingo
and of the Quattro Provveditori together with the
title of the book therein contained.[1]

After this first step progress was rapid. A Camarlingo, moved by the perhaps somewhat un-
monastic ambition of handing down his form and
features to posterity, caused his portrait to be
painted seated at a table or counter *(banco)*
whereon were books and money—the position,
in fact, which he had occupied daily during his
term of office; and the example once set, was
followed by his successors. Thus the earliest Tavolette which we possess may be divided into two

---

[1] L. MUSSINI, *Le Tavolette della Biccherna e della Gabella,*
op. cit. in list of authorities on page 13 supra.

PLATE III.

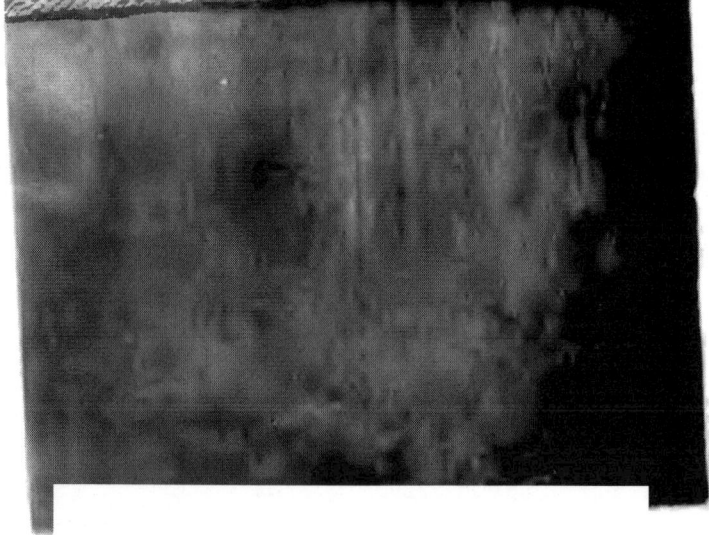

classes, those belonging to the Quattro Provveditori and those belonging to the Camarlinghi.
On the former are inscribed the names of the
Provveditori, accompanied by their coats of arms,
blazoned according to the heraldic art (Plate III);
on the latter are the figures of the Camarlinghi
(Plate IV). In both cases a chronological in-
dication is added which sometimes takes the form
of a definite date, and sometimes consists merely
of a reference to the Potestà who was then in
office. More often both indications are combined.
Almost invariably, the lower half of the Tavolette
are left bare, the inscriptions, the coats of arms
and the portraits being crowded into the upper
portion and terminating with the connecting strap.

Little by little, however, these unpretentious
compositions gave place to pictures of greater
artistic merit and of more elaborate design. The
eternal Camarlingo became wearisome ; and, in
the first half of the XIVth century, we encounter
Tavolette painted with figures of Saints and Angels,
scriptural subjects and allegories; while, later on,
we have representations of actual historical events.
The first signs of the coming change manifested
themselves shortly after the creation of the Magistracy of Gabella, when the officials of Biccherna,
perhaps urged thereto by the fear that the covers
of the books of the new office might surpass their
own in beauty, began to keep one of their registers in Italian instead of Latin and on paper
instead of parchment. The other book was written,

3

as of old, in Latin, and from thenceforward it alone was covered with Tavolette ; so that the money which up to that time had been spent on the embellishment of two books was now able to be devoted to one.[1]   Upon that one were inscribed the names both of the Camarlingo and of the Provveditori, while the entire surface of the Tavoletta was used for decorative purposes.   The first example which we have of this change is to be seen in the Tavoletta of 1314.   There, on the left hand portion of the upper half, is depicted the Camarlingo ; to the right are the arms of the Provveditori, while the lower half is completely occupied by the inscription (Plate V).

A new departure was made towards the middle of the XVth century, when, the use of paper having well nigh superseded that of parchment, the registers of Biccherna began to be made of the former material and to be bound in leather

---

[1] The reader will remember that at first the usual price paid for painting a Tavoletta was 5 *soldi* (see note 5 on page 23 supra). For the first Tavoletta di Gabella which remains to us 7 *soldi* were paid :

1291. *Item vij sol. a Massarucio dipegnitore perchè dipense e' libro de' Signori de la cabela a loro arme.*

In 1307 we have a more elaborate Tavoletta di Gabella which is painted over its entire surface, and this is followed by the Tavoletta di Biccherna of 1314, for which 1 *lira* was paid : *Ancho j lib., dipegnitura el libro de l'entrata e de l'uscita, el quale rimane in Biccherna.*

In 1334 the officials of Gabella paid 2 *lire* for their Tavolettta : *E dèmo per facitura questo libro e per dipegnare. L. ij :* while in 1411 a law was passed limiting the Magistrates of each office to *unum florenum auri pro quolibet libro, non obstante quod in huiusmodi libris fieri soleant maior expensa* (Stat. n. 39, c. 14).

or vellum. Thereupon the officials, being no longer able to paint the covers of their books, had recourse, for a few years, to mural decorations. In 1445, the Quattro Provveditori employed Sano di Pietro to depict the Coronation of the Madonna upon one of the walls of their office in the Palazzo Pubblico (Plate I); while, in the following year, the same master filled up the space which his previous work had left bare with the figures of San Pietro Alessandrino, the Blessed Ambrogio Sansedoni and the Blessed Andrea Gallerani.[1]

Subsequently there was a return to the old system; but since there was no longer any question of using the Tavolette as covers for books, the connecting strap ceased to exist, and they became pictures pure and simple. As such their size was of no great importance, and, while they still continued to bear the date and titles of the registers with which they were synchronous, they gradually grew larger and larger, until from *tavolette* they became *tavole,* and at last were painted upon canvas instead of wood. Indeed, the only features which they any longer possessed which might be supposed to connect them with the offices to which they belonged were to be found in the coats of arms of the Camarlinghi and of the Provveditori or Esecutori.

---

[1] It will be noticed that the inscriptions below these pictures record the names of the officials of Biccherna at whose request they were painted.

Before leaving this branch of our subject it may be remarked that the affreschi of Sano di Pietro, above referred to, are not the only mural pictures which the officials of Biccherna have bequeathed to us, since in the two rooms which constituted their office, we see depicted many interesting episodes of the history of Siena and of Italy, as well as certain biblical subjects. Even in the XIV'th century they had (as we learn from an entry in their books of 30 June 1352) paid to Lippo di Vanni the sum of *l.x.x.xv lib. xvj sol. viij den., pro pictura quam fecit in Biccherna, videlicet Coronatio Nostre Domine.* Of this work a record still exists in the legend visible below the newer affresco of Sano di Pietro: *Lippus Vannis de Senis fecit hoc opus sub anno Domini millesimo trecentesimo lij.* Moreover in 1344 the officials of Gabella employed Ambrogio Lorenzetti to paint an *Annunciation* upon a tavola the dimensions of which were far too large for a book cover. This work will be found in the Accademia delle Belle Arti (Stanza II, no. 33). It is known by the name of the " Madonna de' Donzelli " since it was an object of special veneration among the servitors of the Palazzo. At the foot of the picture is the following inscription : XVII. DI DICEBRE M. CCC. XL. IIII. FECE AMBRVOGIO LOREZI QVESTA TAVOLA ERA CAMARLENGO DO FRACESCO MONACO DI SA GALGANO — E ASSECVTORI BIDO PETRVCCI GIOVANI DI MEO BALDINOTTI MINO DI ADREOCCIO. SCRITTORE AGNOLO LOCTI.

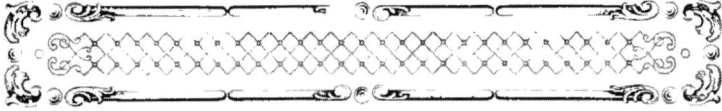

N studying the Tavolette we may conveniently follow the example of Professor Paoli who groups them together under three periods, namely : 1) the thirteenth and fourteenth centuries ; 2) the fifteenth century, and 3) the sixteenth century. The collection ends with six Tavole and two pictures on canvas belonging to the seventeenth century ; but, for our present purpose, these may be ignored since not only do they show a sad decadence in art, but are of little or no historical importance.

And first of

The Tavolette
of the XIIIth and XIVth Centuries.

The Tavolette belonging to this period are 24 in number, namely 19 of Biccherna and 5 of Gabella. With one exception all of the latter belong to the fourteenth century, whereas no fewer than ten of the former are anterior to that date.

The general characteristics of this first period are as follows. A few Tavolette of the thirteenth century are without other ornament than the coats of arms of the Provveditori, but the majority of both centuries display the figure of the Camarlingo, either alone or accompanied by his notary *(scrittore di Biccherna).* In the XIVth century, as I have said, the pictures of Saints begin, together with some allegorical compositions.

The most ancient Tavoletta which remains to us antedates by two years the Battle of Montaperti. It was painted by Maestro Gilio di Pietro, and represents a monk of San Galgano in a white dress, seated in profile on a chair. In his hands he holds a book (Plate IV). Like the work of Dietisalvi who painted several of these portraits, it reveals no sensible progress in the art of the time, and is chiefly interesting as affording us some idea of the appearance of that Don Ugo, who was nine times elected Camarlingo of Biccherna, and whose name is familiar to us in connection with the steps taken for the construction of a fortress in Montepulciano during the Potesteria of Provenzano Salvani. For the rest there is little to be said with regard to the Tavolette containing the portraits of Camarlinghi. Typical figures, if we consider them in the aggregate, they have individually no great importance either from an artistic or historical stand-point. It may,

however, be pointed out that the Tavolette of 1393 and 1394 are worthy of some study since they afford us an excellent idea of the internal arrangements of the offices of Biccherna. There we see the partitions which prevented more than one person from approaching the Camarlingo at a time; the seat reserved for the four Provveditori, and the strong chests for the safe-keeping of documents and of money.

Of religious subjects we have a *San Galgano* of 1320, a *Nativity* of 1334,[1] a *Circumcision* of 1357, a *Holy Trinity* of 1367.

In the first of these, the kneeling figure is the Camarlingo Don Stefano of San Galgano. With regard to the position of the rock into which the Saint has struck his sword, it is to be observed that it is the same as in the device adopted by the Abbey to which he gave his name — a sword standing upright in a rock between two trees. This the monks carved upon their *palazzo apresso a la Maddalena,* which may still be seen in the Via Romana. The shield above the head of San Galgano contains the arms of the Potestà, Count Ugo da Battifolle. The four shields to the right, of course, contain the arms of the Provveditori.

---

[1] One of the *Storie* of an altar piece in the Galleria delle Belle Arti (Stanza I, n. 15) which is evidently by the same painter, is a *Nativity*. The details are almost identical even to the little black devil which, in the Tavoletta, we see departing from the resentful-looking Joseph.

In the Tavoletta of 1334 the coats of arms of the Esecutori appear for the first time below the connecting strap.

These religious subjects, although, no doubt, of less interest than the allegorical Tavolette of 1344 and 1385, have still a distinct historical value, and should by no means be ignored simply because, in their present somewhat dilapidated condition, they do not greatly please the eye. Rightly considered, they serve to remind us of the fact that the life of the Middle Ages dissevered from its superstitions would be as incomprehensible as the *Iliad* without its contending deities, *Paradise Lost* without its Satan, or the twentieth century without its railways, its Röntgen rays and its wireless telegraphy.

Heaven and hell were very real to the men of those days, and the saints were very accessible and very human—easily angered and easily cajoled. Was it not a matter of common knowledge that St. Francis of Assisi had received the stigmata and that Christ Himself had appeared to St. Catherine and exchanged his heart for hers? Did not San Galgano behold the twelve apostles on M. Siepi, and was not his sword still to be seen miraculously imbedded in the rock? Did not Our Lady spread her white and luminous mantle over the Sienese host on the eve of the glorious victory of Montaperti; and did she not, for all her divine motherhood, retain so much of earthly weakness and of female vanity, that Duccio was not afraid to ap-

peal to her for favour because he had painted her
so radiantly lovely?

The existence of the celestial powers and their
intervention in human affairs were facts to be
calculated upon and allowed for; and thus the
religion of the XIIIth and XIVth centuries was,
in one way, extremely sincere. It may not have
led to virtuous living—if a man was not a mis-
creant, a misbeliever, that was of quite secondary
importance—but it did lead to a very constant
and vivid realization of the superhuman, while, in
some sort, men followed the maxim of the Apostle,
and, whatsoever they did in word or deed, did
all in the name of the Lord. The sessions of
their Councils were opened in God's name; their
statutes were compiled *in nomine patris et filii
et spiritus sancti* or *ad honorem dei et beate Virginis et omnium Sanctorum et Sanctarum dei;*
their first care was to legislate for the protection
and maintenance of the *loca venerabilia et religiosa;* they slew their enemies and prosecuted
their vengeances in the name of the Almighty
and for His honour;[1] while, often enough, they
wasted valuable time, which might have been used
for warlike preparations, in making useless pro-
cessions and offering up unavailing prayers.[2]

---

[1] See, for example, DEL LUNGO, *Una vendetta in Firenze* in
Dal Secolo e dal Poema di Dante (Bologna, N. Zanichelli, 1898),
pages 127-128.

[2] Compare DINO COMPAGNI, *Cronica fiorentina*, II, XIII; I. DEL
LUNGO, *Da Bonifazio VIII ad Arrigo VII, pagine di storia fiorentina* (Milano, U. Hoepli, 1899), pages 46-47.

Under these circumstances we cannot wonder that the universal sentiment of the age left a deep impression upon its art, or that the Sienese painters of the XIVth century should have proclaimed themselves, in the opening words of their statute, *per la gratia di Dio manifestatori agli uomini grossi che non sanno lectera, de le cose miracolose operate per virtù et in virtù de la sancta fede.*[1] With the Sienese " religious feeling was a passion on a par with all the other movements of their quick and mobile temperament; it needed ecstatic art for its interpretation." What was cold and sober would not satisfy them, and so it came to pass " that a city famed like Siena for its vanity, its factious quarrels, and its delicate living, produced an almost passionately ardent art of piety." [2] And thus too it is that when we find the Camarlinghi of Biccherna embellishing the covers of their books of account with figures of saints and causing themselves to be depicted as kneeling in adoration before them, there is nothing strange or in-

---

[1] *Breve dell'Arte de' Pittori senesi dell' anno MCCCLI*, published by G. MILANESI in his *Documenti per la storia dell'arte senese* (Siena, O. Porri, 1854), vol. I, page 1. — " It was," says Mr. BERENSON, " the chief business of the mediæval artist to re-write the stories of the Saviour, and of His immaculate Mother, in pictographs so elaborate that even the most unlettered could read them. At the same time these pictographs were intended to be offered up as a sacrifice, along with all the rest of the furnishing and actual decoration of God's holy house, and for this they were to be as resplendent as gold and skill could make them."—*The Central Italian Painters of the Renaissance*, pages 18-19.

[2] J. A. SYMONDS, *Renaissance in Italy, The Fine Arts* (London, 1877), pages 220-221.

consistent about the matter. Rather is it a perfectly natural and normal manifestation of the prevalent ideas of the period in which they lived; and these ideas it is necessary that we should recognize unless we are content to wholly misinterpret much of the history of the Middle Ages.

Moreover the old superstitions died hard. Even in the XVIth century, when the classical revival had transformed the world, when men had returned in all sincerity and faith to the glory and gladness of nature, when the Protestant Reformation had raised almost half of Christendom against the Pope, Siena still faithfully trod the old paths. As often as danger threatened or was averted; whenever enemies invaded her borders or friends gained a victory; if pestilence ravaged the dominion or inclement seasons gave warning of coming scarcity, the ancient credulity revived. As if moved by a common impulse, the entire populace clad themselves in garments of penitence and went in procession through the streets, or hurried, in holiday attire, to join in public festivals of thanksgiving. By the command of the Government gifts were made to the thirty odd convents of the city and its environs, rich offerings were borne in solemn pomp to the churches, bonfires were lighted, cannon were fired and costly religious ceremonies were performed. Praise was given to heaven if things went well, its aid implored if fortune proved unkind. In eight days only, from April 3 to April 11, 1525, according to the calculations made

by Professor Falletti-Fossati, no fewer than fifty-
three masses were said by the order of the Magnificent College,—a cypher which gives an appall-
ing idea of the vast sums which must have been
wasted upon divine offices, to say nothing of the
money spent on wax candles and oblations; and
this at a time when the public treasury was well
nigh empty.[1]

The earliest Tavoletta painted with a religious
subject is, as we have seen, a San Galgano of 1320;
the last of the series is a San Galgano of 1682.

We now come to two allegorical Tavolette,
both of them representing the *Good Government of Siena*. In the first of these (that of 1344)
we see a figure in the prime of life seated in
majesty upon a throne. At his feet is the she-
wolf suckling the twins, an obvious record of the
legendary origin of the city. His garments are
white and black, the colours of the Commune.
In his right hand he holds a sceptre, in his left
a medallion whereon are depicted the Virgin and
Child adored by two angels, as in the most ancient
civic seal. About his head are the four letters C. S.
C. V., which we may doubtless interpret CIVITAS
SENARVM CIVITAS VIRGINIS. It seems al-

---

[1] C. FALLETTI-FOSSATI, in the second of the two lectures on
the *Principali cause della caduta della Repubblica senese*, which he
delivered in 1883 before the R. Accademia dei Fisiocritici. He bases
his statement on the *Benvoglienti Misc.* in the BIBLIOTECA COMUNALE
DI SIENA. Ms. C. V, 5, page 104, *Del Governo di Siena.*

most superfluous to remark that the subject of
this Tavoletta is the same as that which consti-
tutes the central group in the magnificent affresco
of Ambrogio Lorenzetti in the Sala della Pace.
Indeed an examination of the two pictures makes
it appear highly probable that they are both the
work of the same master. In the latter the ma-
jestic giant of the *Reggimento* towers above all
the other figures in bulk and stature. The virtues
which float above him, and are enthroned beside
him, are his assessors and inspirers—he is king.[1]
In the Tavoletta, on the contrary, he sits alone,
in the utter solitude of complete and unapproached
supremacy; grave, impressive, calm.

Born of the same school, and with the same
allegorical conceits, is the Tavoletta of 1385,
wherein a company of citizens stand to the right
and left of the central figure of Good Government to whom they are bound by means of a
rope which both he and they hold in their hands.
On either side trumpeters blow upon their trumpets
announcing to the world the public felicity. This
use of a rope as a symbol of civic concord is, of

---

[1] See J. A. SYMONDS, *op. cit.*, pages 210-214.—Mr. Berenson,
almost blind to the importance of what he terms " mere illustration",
and bent on exploiting his pet theory of " tactile values", at any cost,
as if they were the alpha and omega of artistic merit, describes these
frescoes as " little more than a painted charade" (*op. cit.*, page 51).
If for him the figures of Lorenzetti be indeed "powerless to speak
for themselves", may this not be due to a lack of that intimate knowledge of and sympathy with mediæval life, which enabled Mr. Symonds to perceive what "a passionate and intense meaning" they
had for the great master who painted them?

course, borrowed from the great fresco of Lorenzetti above referred to; but, if the symbolism is
the same, the events symbolized were essentially
different—a fact for which we might almost be
prepared by the diminished nobility and strength
in the face of the Good Government of 1385, as
compared with that of his predecessor of 1344.
The first is aristocratic, forceful, still; the second,
to say nothing of his narrower shoulders and
meaner form, is almost plebeian in his aspect;
and, if I am not mistaken, his glance is furtive.

During the first half of the century Siena had
been ruled by the great merchant oligarchy of
the Nove [1] who, for many years, displayed as much

---

[1] Two recent English writers have completely misconceived the
character of this magistracy. In *The History of St. Catherine of
Siena and her companions* by A. T. DRANE (Longmans, Green
& Co., 1899) we are informed, on page 9, that " at the period of
St. Catherine's birth the government was in the hands of the *popolani*, or middle-class tradesmen "; while F. WITTS in *The Story of
Catherine of Siena (The "Splendid Lives" series)* calls the Nove
an " Oligarchy of inferior arts " (page 15). The phrase is given
between quotation marks, being evidently copied without enquiry
from some equally ill-informed author.—By the statute of their creation it was provided that the Magistracy of the Nove should be
selected *de bonis et legalibus mercatoribus,* and we should not be
guilty of any great exaggeration if we characterized their government
as a government of merchant princes.—" Ce Peuple qui a conquis le
pouvoir sur les nobles c'est la haute bourgeoisie, composée des plus
riches commerçants et industriels : la masse des petits patrons, des
artisans, des ouvriers en est absolument distincte et n'a pas, dans la
Commune, de véritable influence. Le premier réveil du petit peuple
amènera la chute des Nove ; mais pour l'instant il est hors du champ
politique ". The ruling oligarchy consisted not of " inferior arts ",
but of " l'Art des Marchands proprement dits, c'est-à-dire des ban-
quiers et des gros exportateurs, et l'Art de la Laine ". - J. LUCHAIRE.

patriotic spirit and equity as was possible in the
case of a purely class government. Strong in
their alliance with Florence and the other Guelf
Communes of Tuscany, they grasped the reins of
office more firmly than any who came after them.
The power of the Visconti was still in its cradle;
the great plague had not yet devastated Italy,
and the period of their rule was, in fact, the period
of Siena's greatest well-being. Not without good
reason, therefore, did the Magistrates cause to be
painted in the hall of their residence an allegorical representation of the manifold benefits of peace,
prosperity and glory.

In 1385, on the contrary, peace had fled, and
the streets of the city ran red with blood. In
that very year, to the cry of *Viva la Pace!* the
government of the Riformatori had been overthrown. "And they were broken and cast forth
and evil entreated and imprisoned and slain, on
such wise that the city was bereft of all the *Arti*;
and the Kingdom was benefitted thereby and all
the Marches and the Patrimony: and Pisa was
populated with them.... And so was the city of
Siena wasted and undone, in that more than four
thousand good artisans, citizens of the city, were
driven forth, of whom never did a sixth part return." So writes Neri di Donato; and to the cry

*Le Statut des Neuf Gouverneurs et Défenseurs de la Commune de
Sienne*, Extrait des *Mélanges d'Archéologie et d'Histoire* publiés par
l'École française de Rome, T. XXI. (Rome, Imprimerie de la Paix de
Philippe Cuggiani, 1901), pages 28-29.

of *Viva la Pace,* thus raised, corresponds the symbolical picture of the Tavoletta ; and both the one and the other, viewed in the light of the actual facts, assume the character of a grim and sanguinary jest. In the streets of the city, the sacred name of Peace had been used as a signal for pitiless slaughter, while, in the painting of the Biccherna, the cord in the hands of the " Good Government " does not gather together all the people of Siena, but only joins the faction of the victors by a strong and exclusive bond. The trumpets do not announce peace and happiness, but vomit forth fierce blasts of triumph and of menace to stun the ears of the exiles and the conquered.

To what extent the new Government deserved the epithet " good we may perhaps gather from the records of *Concistoro* of 1390, wherein we read that the Priors, for July and August in that year, paid a fine of 20 *soldi* each, which was inflicted *quod inordinate vixerunt et contra bonos mores, ex eo maxime quia pluries et pluries in mane, antequam missa diceretur, comedebant pepones et fructus, et bibebant, et maxime multum ad exedram, ita quod videbantur ab hominibus desuper Campo.* And these were the chief magistrates of the Republic ! The *Monte del Popolo* had been born, and the democratic evolution was completed.

With all the subservience of the vulgar the rulers of Siena seconded the ambitious designs of Gian Galeazzo. They united with him to make war upon Florence with which they had been at

peace, and often in alliance, since the end of the
preceding century ; and they reaped the reward
of their servility by so completely exhausting the
resources of the Commune that, in the year 1400,
they were fain to accept him as their seignior. It
is true that his rule only lasted for four years, but
it sufficed to show that the minds of the Sienese
were already attuned to servitude ; and the *can-
zone* of Saviozzo da Siena *a laude di Giovan Galeazzo duca di Milano* simply voiced a feeling which
must have been common among men who had
suffered as much as had the Sienese from the evils
of Republican rule. It begins as follows :

> Novella monarchia, giusto signore,
> Clemente padre, insigne, virtuoso,
> Per cui pace e riposo
> Spera trovar la dolce vedovella....

Excessive praise, no doubt ; and partly, as what
comes afterwards demonstrates, inspired by hatred
for the Florentines, that

> detestabil seme
> Nimico di quïete e caritade
> Che dicon *libertade*
> E con più tirannia ha guasto il mondo.

Still it is not unreasonable to suppose that already some of the more thoughtful among the
citizens had begun to perceive what, at a later
period, Guicciardini did not fail to proclaim, that
the subjects of a seignior are, as a whole, freer

than those of a Republic because a Monarchy
" è più comune a tutti. "[1]

> RESPUBLICA—a public thing :
>   A shameful shameless prostitute,
>   Whose lust with one lord may not suit,
> So takes by turns its revelling
>   A night with each, till each at morn
>   Is stripped and beaten forth forlorn,
> And leaves her, cursing her. If she,
>   Indeed, have not some spice-draught, hid
>   In scent under a silver lid.
> To drench his open throat with—he
>   Once hard asleep; and thrust him not
>   At dawn beneath the boards to rot.

It may be remarked that the large number
of coats of arms—there are thirteen of them—
emblazoned upon the Tavoletta of 1385 are due
to the fact that, after the revolution, several of
the officials were removed, their places being filled
by persons devoted to the new government. Those
old Sienese appreciated, as fully as does the modern American politician, the great and patriotic
principle that " to the victors belong the spoils. "

The Tavolette of the XVth Century.

It has often been observed that the Sienese
were slower than their neighbours to feel the in-

---

[1] A. FRANCHETTI, *I primordi delle signorie e delle companie di
ventura,* conferenza tenuta a Firenze nel 1891, pubblicata nella *Vita
italiana nel Trecento* (Milano, Fratelli Treves, 1897), page 52. - As
to Saviozzo da Siena see UGURGIERI, *Le Pompe sanesi,* I, 548.

PLATE V.

LIBBRO · DIFRATE IACOMO DELIUM
LIATI CAMARLINGO · EDIMINO DI
NISSE MEO DICITTA · CECCHO DI
DIONE DISAMARTINO EDIMICHANE
LLO DISCO MARTINO · EDICIAO ARI
GI · DICAMOLLIA · QUATRO POUCOI
THOI DELCOMUEDISIEA DSCI MESI IOU
ALICOMICIARO I RELLUGLIO · M · CCC · XIIII
FINIRO IRE GENAIO ADI DG TUTI ·

fluence of the Renaissance, and that, as a consequence, Sienese art remained almost stationary amid the general progress and development of the other Italian schools, preserving its mediæval character down to the end of the XVth century. Then indeed, the influence of the Umbrian and —to a slighter degree—of the Florentine schools began to penetrate into Siena, followed a little later by that of the Lombard ; and these grafts gave fresh vigour to the old stock without destroying its special characteristics. Of this new phase of Sienese art it has been well said that Sodoma was its Leonardo, Baldassare Peruzzi its Raphael, and Beccafumi its Michael Angelo.[1]

At present, however, we are concerned with the XVth century, during the whole of which the Sienese painters, faithful to the old ideals and the old methods, obstinately closed their minds to the new influences and progressed but little beyond the point which had been reached by the better masters of the preceding period. The causes of this persistent archaism were many and complex ; but, very possibly, one of the most potent of them was to be found in the geographical position of Siena, since it seems capable of demonstration that the Renaissance, while hailed with enthusiasm by the population of the plains, encountered serious obstacles in almost all the hill cities. Then too the splendid traditions

---

[1] C. PAOLI, *Siena*, article in the *Encyclopædia Britannica*, vol. XXII, page 43.

of her ancient art and her rivalry with Florence,
the centre of humanism, may well have tended
to make Siena tenacious of her old ideals, which,
to artists and people alike, seemed to be indis-
solubly connected with the triumph of patriotism
and the glory of the Commune.[1]

Moreover the *Breve dell'Arte de' Pittori Senesi* contained a clause which penalized all foreign
artists desiring to exercise their calling in Siena.
" *Ancho ordeniamo* (so runs chapter XI of that
Statute) *che qualunque dipintore forestiere vorrà
venire affare l'arte ne la città di Siena, che inanzi
che cominci a lavorare, paghi e pagar debbia al-
l' università de' dipintori, ricevendo el camarlengo
per la detta arte, uno fiorino d'oro, e che 'l detto
forestieri debba dare buona et soficiente ricolta in-
fino a la quantità di XXV lire....*"[2] Such a tax
was heavy enough to be practically prohibitive,
and, if beneficial to the pockets of the Sienese
painters, was certainly detrimental to their art,
since so stringent a protection of home industries
must have cut most of them off from any knowledge of the work done by their neighbours, and
thrown them back upon their own resources and
their old models.

Thus the art of Siena, in the XVth century,
was, if not actually retrograde, extremely conser-

---

[1] P. Rossi, *L'arte senese nel Quattrocento*, in the *Bullettino
senese di storia patria*, vol. VI (1899), pages 3 et seq.

[2] G. Milanesi, *Documenti*, op. cit., vol. I, page 5. See also
chap. LII, LIII, page 22.

vative. Nor is the fact one which is altogether to be regretted, because, as Professor Paoli remarks, the antiquated character of the Sienese paintings, separated as they are from every extraneous influence, and full of simplicity and spontaneity, is of itself extremely attractive. If they do not seduce the eye with pretentious compositions, if they show but little appreciation of significance of form, if they sometimes display a narrow and obstinate opposition to every novelty and to every expansion, they nevertheless exercise upon the mind that strange and subtle fascination which is always felt in the presence of those objects and works of art which preserve a character distinctively their own ; and we are forced to regard thoughtfully and reverently pictures so absolutely free from even the most inferential appeal to the coarser passions of humanity, and in which the sentiment of artistic religion is manifested with such ingenuous fervour. Moreover it cannot be denied that, in the works of such artists as Matteo di Giovanni and Benvenuto di Giovanni (at his best), we find beautiful pattern, manifestations of a feeling for rich colour and a sense of sumptuousness which give them a high place in the art of the Quattrocento.

Now in the Tavolette della Biccherna and della Gabella, modest compositions and frankly Sienese, the beauties of this school are far more obvious than its defects ; and among the artists who painted them were some of the most distinguished men of that age. Such were Guidoccio Cozzarelli, Matteo di Giovanni, and Francesco Giorgio Martini who, even in this restricted sphere, displays notable indications of his versatile and daring genius; while, last but not least, we have more than one example of the work of Sano di Pietro—*Ansanus Petri pictor famosus et homo totus deditus Deo* [1] —whom Gaetano Milanesi, not without good reason, praises above all the other Sienese painters of his day. Many he excelled in correctness of design, all in the religious feeling of his work ; and indeed the gentle virginal faces of his Madonnas and the celestial beauty of his seraphim are such as to place him almost on a par with the Blessed Fra Angelico himself.[2]

Moreover, although the technique of the Sienese school [3] had not yet felt the effects of the Renaissance, the thoughts and aspirations of the citizens had undergone a very sensible transformation. It was a period of revolt against all that was narrow and mediæval ; and, if mystic art could still satisfy, it was only satisfying because mysticism and sensuality are sisters ; and in *molles Senæ* there was much corruption.[4] In

---

[1] G. MILANESI, *Documenti,* vol. II, page 390.

[2] *Sulla storia dell' arte toscana* (Siena, tip. Sordo muti, 1873), pages 50-51.

[3] I have no intention of depreciating it. Even those who are least in sympathy with the Primitives admire the excellent technique of the Early Sienese masters which they had received as a priceless inheritance from Simone Martini.

[4] It seems to me that no one who has attentively studied MAX NORDAU's *Degeneration* can well doubt that there is a distinct and

its nobler aspects the XVth century was an epoch of intense effort and of boundless curiosity, fruitful of political changes and of renewed civic and intellectual vigour. The relations of the Commune with her neighbours were enlarged and extended far beyond the limits of Tuscany; events which took place in distant cities and which, a century earlier, would have excited no attention, were now considered as matters of considerable, sometimes of vital interest; the field of Sienese vision was widened until it comprised the whole Peninsula, and thus historical facts suddenly acquired a new importance. This change was early reflected in the Tavolette; representations of actual events began to take the place of allegorical and religious subjects, and long before the old artistic tradition had spent its force, the new spirit of the Renaissance had introduced an essentially human element.

---

well nigh indissoluble connection between mysticism and sensuality. A very startling example of this strange fact is to be found in the *Laudi spirituali del Bianco da Siena*, Laud 50 (I have quoted the verses in question in my work above cited, *The "Ensamples" of Fra Filippo*, &c., pages 238-239); while another quite modern instance exists in Rossetti's *Blessed Damozel*. (See the English translation of *Degeneration*, page 89, edition 1895.)

It is moreover notorious that in the XVIth and XVIIth centuries it was precisely those who "were infected by the sensuous romance of pietism, the superstitious respect for sacraments and ceremonial observances, which had been wrought by the Catholic Revival into ecstatic frenzy," who were filled with "correlative yearnings after sacrilegious debauchery."—J. A. SYMONDS, *Renaissance in Italy, The Catholic Reaction* (London, Smith Elder & Co., 1898), part I, page 328.

There are 26 Tavolette belonging to the XVth century, namely 17 of Gabella and 9 of Biccherna.

In our consideration of this period we may class together the religious and allegorical subjects.

Of the former we have a *S. Pietro Alessandrino* of 1440,[1] and a *St. Michael the Archangel* of 1444, which are generally attributed to Giovanni di Paolo; a *Presentation of the Virgin* of 1484 by Guidoccio Cozzarelli; an *Annunciation* of 1445 in the manner of Giovanni di Paolo, and a *St. Jerome in the desert* of 1436, by an unknown author. The head of the Saint is extremely beautiful.

Of the allegorical Tavolette the following are worthy of special mention : a *Wisdom which emanates from God*—the Σοφία του Θεου of the Epistles—painted by Sano di Pietro in 1471 and a *Government of Siena* of 1474, which, judging,

---

[1] In the catalogue of 1889 this Tavoletta is said to represent *San Niccolò da Bari*, but this, as Signor Lisini has shown, is probably a mistake. On the 16th November 1403, the day dedicated to San Pietro Alessandrino, the Government of the Dodici was overthrown, and in commemoration of this event a solemn annual festival was decreed; while, afterwards, in 1414, to render it more splendid a palio was inaugurated. San Pietro Alessandrino was thus a saint of some importance in Siena, and he was early taken by the Arte degli Speziali as their protector. In the year 1440, the Camarlingo di Gabella was an apothecary—*Antonio di Francesco, speziale*—and he naturally caused the cover of his register to be ornamented with the figure of the patron Saint of his Arte.

among other indications, by the exaggeration of the lines of the face running downward from the nose, should be either a Benvenuto di Giovanni or of his school.[1] In the Tavoletta of 1474, as in those of 1344 and 1385, the central figure is clad in black and white. He holds in his hand a black and white sphere; above his head is the word LIBERTAS which forms the inscription upon one of the shields of the Commune;[2] and starting from his face, as if issuing from his mouth, is the legend KI BEN MINISTRA REMGNA. To his left sits the Camarlingo; to his right the Scrittore. The latter is making an entry in the book before him, while the former turns his head to listen to the words spoken by the allegorical figure.

Very notable, also, is the Tavoletta di Bic-

---

[1] Compare, for example, the three pictures of Benvenuto in the Accademia delle Belle Arti, Stanza X, n. 37, 38, 39.—I should have been inclined to attribute the Tavoletta to Girolamo di Benvenuto if he had been old enough at the period when it was painted, since the mannerism referred to is so strongly marked as to lead to the inference that it is the work of an imitator.

[2] The three shields which we see everywhere blazoned about Siena are:

1) The *balzana,* the party coloured shield, whereof the upper half is white, the lower black. Like the she-wolf suckling the twins, it records the Roman origin of the city.

2) The azure shield with the word LIBERTAS, in letters of gold, running diagonally across it. This is commemorative of Siena's connection with Charlemagne.

3) The Lion rampant—the arms of the People, the *Popolo,* which, be it observed, was quite distinct from the Commune.

As to the legendary origin of these three devices the reader should consult RONDONI, *Tradizioni popolari e leggende di un Comune medioevale e del suo contado,* Firenze, tip. M. Cellini e C., 1886.

cherna of 1437, which seems to belong to the
school of Giovanni di Paolo and of which the
original is preserved in the Museum of Industrial
Art at Berlin.   Here the *Plague* is symbolized in
the form of a demon archer with the wings of
a bat.   He is all black even to his skull-like face,
and is covered with a black garment.   From his
belt hangs a scythe ; he is mounted upon a fu-
riously galloping black horse and is shooting arrows as he comes.   On the ground, beneath the
hoofs of his charger, lie the bodies of four dead
men clothed in bright raiment, red and green and
violet and blue, in sharp contrast with the grizly
shape above them.   The colours are brilliant and
extraordinarily fresh.   The arrows of the archer
are directed towards a group of six persons who
are gathered about a table in the shade of a
portico.   They are intent upon a game played with
three dice—probably zara—and are completely
indifferent to the approaching peril, though the
air is full of flying arrows, one of which seems
to be directed towards the groin, another to the
neck and two to the armpits of various players—
those being the regions where the lumps or bu-
boes, so characteristic of the pestilence, most fre-
quently made their appearance.   These swellings
were often the seat of acute pain like that of a
stab ; and we almost expect, as we look upon the
picture, to see one of the careless gamblers suddenly clutch at the affected part, uttering the while
that despairing cry of the plague-stricken with

which Fra Filippo Agazzari has made us so familiar: *Oimè io mi sento el grosso!* [1]

The players are all young, and one of them is a woman. The typical figure of the *Barattiere* is absent, and we are therefore disposed to infer that the game is a private and illegal one, played *in caupona vel lupanari*—possibly in the house of the woman. She is seated to the right of the table and is clad in red with a yellow head-dress; beside her is a pile of money which she has won from her *vis-à-vis,* who still holds in his hand an empty dice-box. Despair is written upon his face; the game is lost, and the fatal arrow is even now piercing him beneath the arm. [2]

With regard to the symbolism of the picture, it may be of interest to recall the fact that the sufferers in the great plague of Constantinople, in the VIth century, imagined that they were smitten by arrows from the bow of an invisible demon.

The Sienese chroniclers relate that, in the year 1437, from June to the end of December *fu grande moria; e morì grandi cittadini e molti altri.* The city was almost diserted; several of the Priori and other magistrates died, among the rest the Capitano di Giustizia, Messer Carlo *de*

---

[1] See *Assempro* LVII, page 212 of CARPELLINI's edition of *Gli Assempri di Fra Filippo da Siena* (Siena, Gati, 1864).

[2] Of this Tavoletta (the original of which is at Berlin) I have only seen a photograph. For my description thereof I am indebted, at least as far as the colours are concerned, to F. ELLON, *op. cit.*

Saliceto of Bologna.[1]   The frightful rapidity of the spread of the disease appears to be indicated by the fact that the archer of the Tavoletta is actually outrunning and overtaking his arrows.

Almost more notable than the Tavoletta just described is that of 1468, in which Professor Mussini sees the manner of Francesco di Giorgio Martini, but which Mr. Berenson, as I think mistakenly, attributes to Benvenuto di Giovanni. It represents *Peace and War,* not from an ideal stand-point, but as they would appear to a minister of finance having regard to their economic consequences.   In April 1468, Pope Paul II. succeeded in bringing about a general pacification of Italy in which Siena was included.   The event was celebrated with great public rejoicings and, in memory thereof, the officials of Gabella caused this Tavoletta to be painted.   To the left we see a group of citizens who receive money from the public treasury, while above them hovers Peace, a nude female with an olive bough in her hand and the legend HÆC (*pax*) CIVES DITAT.   To the right are soldiers of fortune to whom the Camarlingo tenders their pay.   Overhead is War armed with a sword, and the motto HOC (*bellum*) EXTEROS.

---

[1] In the preceding year the city seems to have been greatly afflicted by earthquakes. *Exinde anno insequenti* (1437) *Pestis ingens Civitatem ac Regionem omnem invasit, ita ut pæne a suis civibus discerretur.   Ex quo factum est ut rapinæ & furta quamplurima per fere vacuam Civitatem committerentur, ac etiam sacra subriperentur* ...... See the *Historia Senensis* in MURATORI, *Rer. Italic. Script.*, XX, *ad annum.*

Not a few allegorical Tavolette are conse-
crated to the Virgin Mary, the *Advocata Senensium*.[1] Of these the earliest is that of 1451, which
is also interesting as forming a connecting link
with the portrait Tavolette of the XIVth century,
representing, as it does, the figure of the Camarlingo di Biccherna, Ghino di Pietro Bellanti. To
the left is the Madonna spreading her mantle over
the city, while to the right we see Misser Ghino
in the act of washing his hands in a basin, assisted
by an attendant who pours water over them out
of a jug. In this year, by a vote of the *Consiglio
del Popolo* of 9th July, it was resolved to once
more substitute ecclesiastical for lay Camarlinghi,
and no doubt the last of the secular officials de-
sired to indicate that he retired from his administration of the public revenues with clean hands.[2]

Much more important is the Tavoletta of 1467.
In this, as in the preceding year, the city was
grievously troubled by earthquakes. The chronicler Tommaso Fecini relates that, in 1466, *a dì
xv agosto incominciarono i tremuoti in Siena e
seguitando ognuno faceva gli alloggiamenti per le
Piazze. In detti dì si fe' una bella processione di-*

---

[1] The Virgin enjoyed a special cult in Siena, which had been
dedicated to her in 1260. The money of the Commune was inscribed
with the legend SENA VETVS CIVITAS VIRGINIS ; and the author of
La città diletta di Maria declares " che non sia giudizio temerario il
giudicar Mistero di Maria in tutte le cose del popolo senese." I have
treated the subject at length in my *Our Lady of August and the
Palio of Siena* (Siena, Enrico Torrini, 1899); and to that work I
refer the reader.

[2] See pages 19-20 supra.

cendo: QUI HABITAT IN ADIVTORIO ALTISSIMI.
*E durorono tanto li detti tremuoti che per li di-
sagi si colse molte infermità e morirono molte
persone da bene.* The same facts are narrated in
in the "Historia Senensis" published by Muratori in vol. XX. of his "Rerum Italicarum Scrip-
tores": *Terræmotus ingentes hoc anno fuere, qui
circa Augusti mensis finem incipientes, per dies
viginti perduravere, tanto mortalium terrore, ut
in plateas plurimi dormitum exirent, ita ut pro
incommodo multi languoribus afficerentur.*

Of the following year Allegretto Allegretti
records that " on the 22nd day of August, the
same being Saturday, at two hours of night,[1]
there was a very great earthquake which was
followed by others less violent, on such wise that
every man departed from his house; and the folk
betook themselves to the Piazze and to the gardens,
abiding there as best they were able ; and they
made many booths and tents and houses of wood;
and often there came great and little shocks. And
on the third day of September there was one so
great that all men were dismayed thereat, and
two of the coats of arms of the battlements of
the Uffiziali della Mercanzia, which were toward
the Campo, fell, but, thanks be to God, no man
was hurt thereby. Now many deem that these
earthquakes have befallen by reason of the great

---

[1] *A ore due di notte.*—Since at the end of August the sun sets
at about seven o'clock, "two hours of night" would be 9 p. m. according to our reckoning.

heat which hath been for divers months, and by
reason of the great drought in that never hath it
rained ; others say that this thing hath come upon
us for our sins, the which is more believable. "

Naturally, in such straits as these, the Sienese
turned for aid to the celestial powers, and in 1467
Francesco di Giorgio Martini painted, upon a Tavoletta di Biccherna, *the Madonna protecting the
City of Siena in the time of Earthquakes*—AL
TENPO DE TREMVOTI.   Here the Virgin is depicted on high, among the angels, while round
about the city are erected those *Trabacche e Pa-
diglioni e Case di legname* of which Allegretto
Allegretti speaks ; and indeed, if we may credit
the story told by Girolamo Gigli, the Sienese
undoubtedly owed their deliverance to the direct
interposition of heaven, vouchedsafe after they had
appealed for help to a " miraculous Image of the
Great Mother of God which at that time was
manifested near Viterbo in an oak." Wherefore,
in September when the earthquakes had ceased,
the Signoria sent twelve of the principal citizens
with a votive offering *alla miracolosa Immagine
della Madonna della Quercia in Viterbo ;* and,
for a perpetual memorial thereof, a picture was
painted in the hall of the Palace of that town,
representing the twelve Sienese humbly kneeling
to offer their city to the Virgin.   Below is the
following inscription : *Inclita Senarum urbs cen-
tenis sexque denis diris terremotibus plane libe-
rata grata et pia illius Respublica missis huc,*

voti causa, proceribus suis mensam argenteam suæ urbis Effigiem referentem huic Deiparæ dono dat: salutis anno 1467.[1]

It may possibly be of interest to note that, even as I write, the picture of the Madonna del Voto, " she who hearkened unto the people of Siena what time the Florentines were routed at Montaperto," stands unveiled in the Duomo, in order that through her intercession the rain may cease. For weeks, ever since Siena was delivered into the hand of Satan by reason of the order which went forth for the demolition of the Convent of the Cappuccine, there has been an almost uninterrupted downpour. Rome is flooded for our sins, and the good Sienese watch with trembling expectation the workman who first struck his impious pick into the sacred edifice, for assuredly the wrath of God must smite him and he will fall dead suddenly. Only this morning (Sunday, February 16th) was our Lady unveiled, and now, as I lay down my pen at midnight and open my window, I see free sky and stars. The *Advocata Senensium* is as powerful as ever, or the priests who serve her are singularly good judges of an approaching change of weather.

Another Tavoletta of the same class is that of Gabella of 1489, wherein five citizens (probably the Camarlingo and the four Esecutori) are rep-

---

[1] GIGLI, *Diario senese* (second edition), vol. II, pag. 182. Compare the same author's *La città diletta di Maria* (Siena, tip. all'insegna di Santa Caterina, 1873), pages 26-27.

resented as kneeling outside one of the gates of Siena, clad in the garb of penitence. The Virgin approaches them bearing in her arms the infant Redeemer, whom, by their gestures, the five appear to be entreating to enter their city. From the action of her hand and the way in which her face is turned toward her Son, it is evident that the Divine Mother is seconding the prayer of the suppliants. Nor can the result be doubtful; the baby arms of the Christ are already extended towards the gateway.

And now, although we have by no means exhausted even such of the allegorical and religious Tavolette as refer to the Madonna in her character of *Advocata Senensium,* we may, for the moment, turn our attention to the historical subjects, since, if these be treated in their chronological order, almost all the more important of the remaining Tavolette, whether religious or allegorical, will be found to assume their proper places in our pictorical chronicle.

The two greatest names which are connected with the history of Siena during the XVth century are, if we exclude San Bernardino, unquestionably those of the Emperor Sigismund and of Æneas Sylvius Piccolomini, Pope Pius II.
In 1432, the former halted in Siena on his way to Rome and passed more than ten months there while he negotiated as to the terms of his

5

coronation. He received a most princely welcome and his personality seems to have made a deep impression upon the Sienese. At any rate his portrait appears upon the Cathedral Pavement where it is, as Mr. Cust observes, " the only picture which is neither biblical, symbolical nor heraldic," [1] and his coronation at the hands of Eugenius IV. (21 May 1433) is depicted in the earliest extant Tavoletta of the century. Unfortunately the left hand portion of the painting is greatly damaged and we are unable to see the knights and gentlemen who formed the retinue of the Emperor—among them, perhaps, that same Eurialo whose loves have been so vividly described for us in the *Storia di due Amanti*—but the face of Sigismund himself is sufficiently clear, and it may interest the visitor to Siena to compare these two contemporary presentments of him with the following description from the facile pen of Æneas Sylvius Piccolomini: *Fuit autem Sigismundus egregiæ staturæ, illustribus oculis, fronte spaciosa, genis ad gratiam rubescentibus, barba prolixa et copiosa....* The rest of the passage I omit as it refers rather to his intellectual and moral than to his physical characteristics.[2]

The Tavoletta which I have just mentioned is of Biccherna and was painted in 1433. In

---

[1] R. H. H. Cust, *The Pavement Masters of Siena* (London, George Bell & Sons, 1901), page 76.

[2] The entire passage, together with a translation, will be found in the late Dr. Creichton's *History of the Papacy* (London, Longmans Green & Co., 1897), vol. II, pages 316-317.

the preceding year the officials of Gabella had caused the Emperor to be depicted seated upon a throne at the door of the Palazzo Pubblico, surrounded by barons and dignitaries of the Empire, while the Magistrates of the Republic swore fealty to him on the Gospels. Below were the following verses :

> Nel millequattrocento trenta due,
> Regnando nell' uffitio di Ghabella,
> Sigismondo Imperadore aSsiena fue
> Cho' gente magna, gratiosa et bella ;
> A piè el Palazzo di questa cittade
> Volse la fede et dècci libertade.

This Tavoletta is now lost, but in the days of Pecci it was, as he informs us, preserved in the office of Gabella.[1]

The glories of Pius II. are illustrated by no fewer than three Tavolette, while it is probable that a fourth (that of 1449) representing the *Coronation of Nicolas V.* may owe its existence to the fact that Æneas Sylvius, who was then the representative of the Emperor in Rome, had taken a keen interest in the exaltation of Tommaso Parentucelli. Not only had he been chosen custodian of the Conclave, but, at the request of the

---

[1] See the Ms. of GIOVANNI ANTONIO PECCI, *Raccolta d' iscrizioni e di armi senesi,* of which Signor LISINI has made much use in his list of Tavolette now scattered or lost, but of which record remains to us (*op. cit.,* pages XXXVII et seq.).

newly-elected Pope, he had carried the cross at his coronation (18 March 1447). At the time the Tavoletta was painted a Piccolomini was one of the Provveditori, and it was probably at his suggestion that the officials of Biccherna thus commemorated the honourable part played by their fellow-citizen upon that occasion.

In 1455 Nicolas was succeeded by Calixtus III. Less than two years before Constantinople had fallen into the hands of the Turks, and the new Pope was filled with a devouring zeal for prosecuting the war against the infidels. " He solemnly committed to writing his inflexible determination. ' I, Pope Calixtus, vow to Almighty God and the Holy Trinity that by war, maledictions, interdicts, excommunications, and all other means in my power, I will pursue the Turks, the most cruel foes of the Christian name.' With this object in view Calixtus III. sent legates to every country to quicken the zeal of Christendom; " [1] and in Siena, as the chronicler Tommaso Fecini tells us, *a dì v d'aprile frate Giovanni di Santo Spirito per comandamento di papa Calisto fe' fare in tre dì, divote processioni, e fe' vestire di bianco fanciulli e fanciulle con croci rosse in petto e ghirlande d'olivo in testa ; e il terzo dì sterno chiuse le buttighe e i Padrini co' loro popolani e con loro e' vestiti a bianco della loro Parrocchia tutti per le perdonanze : e il tutto perchè il turco non prosperasse.*

---

[1] CREICHTON, *op. cit.*, vol. III, page 180.

Of this incident we have a record in a Tavoletta di Gabella of 1455 by an unknown artist,
representing *the Annunciation*. On high, seated
upon a cloud, with her arms meekly crossed upon
her breast and with an open book upon her knees,
is the Virgin, while the Angel of the Lord bows
before her, as he pronounces the words: " Hail,
thou that art highly favoured." On the right and
on the left stand gigantic figures. That to the
left is St. Bernard of Clairvaux, whose father per-
ished in the first crusade, and who himself, after
the capture of Edessa, preached a second holy
war, and by his marvellous eloquence kindled
anew the crusading madness throughout France
and Germany. To the right is Pope Calixtus in
pontifical robes, in the act of blessing the kneeling
multitude of youths and maidens, clothed in white,
with red crosses upon their shoulders, and olive
garlands upon their heads.

It is curious to note that Siena possesses
another picture of this Pope, and that there, as in
the Tavoletta, he is represented in the presence of
our Lady who recommends her beloved city to
his care. On two scrolls are written the words
spoken by the Virgin and the reply of Calixtus :

O PASTOR DEGNO AL MIO POPOL CRISTIANO
A TE DI SIENA ORMAI LA CVRA RENDO
FA CH ALLEI VOLGA OGNI TVO SENSO HVMANO

VERGINE MADRE A DIO CARA CONSORTE
SEL TVO CALISTO È DEGNO A TANTO DONO
A SIENA NON TORRAMMI ALTRO CHE MORTE.

Below we see a number of mules entering the gates of Siena. They are loaded with grain sacks marked with the *Balzana*. At the foot is the legend CALISTVS III SANVS PETRI DE SENIS PINXIT. This picture, which was formerly in the Palazzo Pubblico, is now to be seen in the Accademia delle Belle Arti (Stanza IV, n. 20).

We may just mention a Tavoletta di Biccherna of 1457 by Sano di Pietro, symbolical of the peace made between the Sienese Republic and the Count Iacomo Piccinino, and pass on to the three Tavolette which refer to Pius II.

Of these two belong to 1460, while the third was not painted until the last year of the century. In the first is represented the *Coronation of Pius II.;* in the second we see the Pope investing his nephew, Francesco Todeschini (afterwards Pius III.), with the cardinal's hat; while, in the Tavoletta of 1499, which depicts *St. Catherine receiving the Stigmata,* Pius II. appears seated in an alcove and holding in his hand a scroll with the legend STIMATA PASSA FVIT. By her canonization (June 1461) he gratified his love for Siena. He tells us that he dictated the Bull himself.

Assisting at the *Coronation of Pius II.* is the Virgin. The Pope, a pathetic figure looking weary and feeble, is seated between two cardinals who set the tiara upon his head. The painting is generally attributed to Giovanni di Paolo, but Mr. Berenson believes it to be a Vecchietta. It is probably a portrait. Within two circles, in the

upper corners of the Tavoletta and occupying the
space to the right and left of the Madonna, are
to be seen the Imperial Eagle and the blended
arms of the People and the Commune—the *Balzana* and the Lion. Below the picture of the coronation is the city of Siena, outside whose walls
prowl two chimæras, lion-headed and dragon-
tailed, possibly intended to symbolize the dangers
to which the popular government was exposed
by the elevation to the Papacy of a citizen so
hostile to the exclusive predominance of the bour-
geois element as was Æneas Sylvius.[1]

It would be irrelevant in this place to discuss
the affreschi of Pinturicchio in the Libreria del
Duomo ; but it is perhaps worth while mentioning
that there is another picture of Pius II., which
connects itself with the Tavolette since it was
painted in the office of Biccherna in the Palazzo
Pubblico. It is a work of no artistic merit, but
it represents the great Sienese Pope as we like
to think of him beneath the chestnut shades of
Monte Amiata.

We now pass to the year 1479, when, after
the failure of the Pazzi conspiracy, Pope Sixtus IV.
having leagued himself with Ferrante of Naples
and with the Sienese, the allies invaded the Florentine territory. We have one record of this
campaign in the *Sala del Mappamondo* of the
Palazzo Pubblico, where Francesco di Andrea and

---

[1] See MALAVOLTI, *Historia*, parte III, lib. IV, c. 60 et seq.

Giovanni di Cristofano painted the affresco of the
victory of Poggio Imperiale ;[1] while a second is
to be found in that Tavoletta di Gabella which
represents the triumphal entry of the allied army
into Colle di Val d' Elsa.

At Poggio the Florentines had fled like sheep.
"Never," says Ammirato,[2] "befel any rout more
dastardly than this, in that scarcely was the battle
joined when our folk turned and fled." But Colle
made a gallant defence, women and men alike
fought in the breaches which the cannon of the
besiegers had made in their walls, and four times
they repelled the assailants with great slaughter,
"so that, besides the dead, the number of the
wounded and maimed was such that of a surety
all the hospitals of Siena were filled with them."[3]
When they were no longer able to defend the
Borgo, the Colligiani set it on fire and retired
into the Castello where they held out until the
middle of November. On the 12th they agreed
to surrender if the Florentines did not succeed
in raising the siege before the night of the 14th.
No help came, and on the 15th the allied army
entered the city. The following passage from the
Chronicle of Tommaso Fecini will serve to further
illustrate the event: *A dì xxiiij si pose campo a*

---

[1] S. BORGHESI e L. BANCHI, *Nuovi documenti per la storia del-
l' arte senese* (Siena, Torrini, 1898), page 226.

[2] AMMIRATO, *Istorie Fiorentine* (Firenze, Batelli e Co., 1818),
tom. V, page 240.

[3] *Ibid.*, page 246.

Colle di Valdelsa, e li v'andò le bombarde e fessi uno bello e grande Campo et era fornito et abbondante di vettovoglie. In pochi dì s'affossò il Borgo di sopra e la Indiavolata (the name of one of the bombardes) *faceva gran flagello di case, le due e tre per volta. A dì xij di Novembre a xj ore sonò a gloria, chè Colle s'era dato a patti, tre dì e a xv venne l'olivo e féssi gran festa.*[1]

This war was brought to an end by the peace of 13 March 1480. Thereupon Alfonso, Duke of Calabria, who had captained the allied forces, attempted to make himself seignior of Siena The Noveschi favoured his pretensions and many of the people sided with them. On the 22nd of June they rose in revolt and, aided by the Duke's sol diery, reorganized the government to their own advantage. Dividing the power between their two orders of the Nove and the Popolo, they excluded the Riformatori and replaced them by a new and heterogeneous order styled the *Aggregati,* composed of nobles, exiles of 1456, and citizens of other orders who had never before been in office. It was a year of turmoil and uncertainty; men's hearts failed them for fear, and none knew what the morrow might bring forth. To this condition of things we owe the Tavoletta of Gabella which represents the Virgin recommending the troubled city to the tender mercies of her Divine Son

---

[1] As to the *Feste senesi per la presa di Colle d'Elsa,* see the article of F. BANDINI-PICCOLOMINI in the *Miscellanea storica senese,* vol. IV (1896), pages 129-132.

(Plate VI). She is depicted as kneeling before a miniature Siena raised upon three columns, around which she draws a rope, the ancient symbol of civic concord. Her face is singularly sweet and youthful. In her right hand she holds a scroll upon which is inscribed the legend HEC EST CIVITA (*sic*) MEA. Overhead, among the clouds, the Redeemer bends forward to receive her prayer. Mr. Berenson is of opinion that this picture is the work of Neroccio di Landi ; Signor Lisini attributes it to Francesco di Giorgio Martini.

Three years later the Noveschi were deprived of the government, and, under colour of a general pacification, all the Orders or *Monti* were reduced to one only called *del Popolo*. To give a religious sanction to this fact Siena was dedicated to the Virgin according to the ancient ritual and the keys of the city were presented to her in the Duomo. This ceremony is depicted in a Tavoletta di Gabella of 1483, where the Virgin is represented as leaning forward to receive the keys at the hand of the Prior. Beneath the picture and above the coats of arms of the officials we read the following inscription APREXENTATIONE DE LE CHIAVI QVANDO TVTTI E QVATRO E MONTI S'ADVSSENO AD VNO. But not for that did civic discord cease, and, at last, things came to such a pass that, as Allegretto Allegretti declares, " good men were not able to speak nor to blame that which was done amiss, because the government was in the hands of certain lewd follows of the

PLATE VI.

baser sort (*alcuni popolari di mala vita*) who, albeit they were but few, were more powerful, few
and evil as they were, than the other citizens
who were good; " and this, as Signor Lisini
suggests, may be the reason why, in 1485, the
officials of Gabella caused a Tavoletta to be painted
with the *Sacrifice of Isaac,* since, in those years
of suspicion and violence, the selection of any
subject which could have been twisted into a political allusion might have been fraught with some
danger.

In 1487 the Noveschi returned glorious and
triumphant with Pandolfo Petrucci at their head.
They easily dispersed the few adherents of the
Popolo who offered resistence; the Captain of the
People was slain, and the government was reorganized. The public books record these events
as being brought about *per gratia di Dio et della
sua gloriosa madre Vergine Maria signora di
questa città ;*[1] and, for a memorial of so auspicious
an occasion, the conquerors caused to be painted
upon a Tavoletta di Gabella a ship bearing the
arms and banners of the Commune, which the
Virgin, clad all in gold and surrounded by cherubs,
guides with her hand upon the bowsprit into the
still waters of a haven beside which rise the walls
and towers of Siena. And so, with constant change,
we see the celestial patronage adapt itself to the

---

[1] ARCH. DI STATO IN SIENA, *Delib. del Consiglio generale della
campana del 27 luglio 1487.*—Compare C. PAOLI, *Del magistrato di
Balìa nella Repubblica di Siena* (Siena, Bargellini, 1879), page 22.

pleasure of opposing factions, according to the
temporary predominance of each.

For nearly a quarter of a century Siena enjoyed peace and prosperity under the domination
of Pandolfo Petrucci, a great and able statesman,
who, if magnificence be not merely physical and
sensuous but rather intellectual and moral, richly
deserved his title of *il Magnifico*. He left the
established forms of government intact and, if he
acquired despotic authority, acquired it only by
virtue of his strength of character and the con-
tinual increase of his personal influence. Fate
called him to play his part upon a narrow stage
and to a limited audience, but he displayed qual-
ities which might have graced the mightiest mon-
arch. Above all he fully realized, what is often
forgotten but what is in fact axiomatic, that the
first duty of a ruler is to rule; and he was virile
enough not to shrink from bloodshed when it was
necessary for the preservation of his authority.
That he should have displayed an over scrupulous
respect for the lives of his enemies would have
stamped him as a man of another age, born out
of due season; and his early life had not been
such as to soften his character. Undoubtedly
the instinct of self preservation had much to do
with his inflexible determination to suppress opposition at any cost, but it was probably combined
with higher motives. The murder of his father-
in-law, Niccolò Borghesi (1500), has often been
spoken of as a serious blot upon his fair fame;

but I submit, on the contrary, that it may be
fairly regarded as a deed of the highest patriotism.
Pandolfo was not naturally cruel, but he knew
only too well that nothing but his seigniory stood
between the commune and the old " chronic condition of wild, whirling faction-fight " which was
rapidly reducing Siena to impotence and making
her a by-word throughout the world.[1]   Therefore when Niccolò Borghesi conspired against him,
Niccolò Borghesi had to be removed.   That the
method adopted for his taking off was the dagger
of the assassin should hardly be allowed to affect
our judgment.   In those days even Popes and
Cardinals were far from being squeamish about
such matters; and certainly no man could hope
to effectually serve the State unless " careless of
justice or injustice, of mercy or cruelty, of honour
or disgrace, he was willing to save his fatherland
rather than his own soul." [2]

Nor (*pace* Burckhardt) are we without some
reason for believing that, even if Pandolfo was
not such a patriot, he at least as nearly approached
that high ideal as any man of his time.   At any
rate the question is disputable; [3] and, in view of

---

[1] See, for example, the often quoted statement of PHILIPPE DE
COMINES, *Mémoires,* livr. VIII, chap. 3 ; and compare FALLETTI-
FOSSATI, *Principali cause della caduta della Repubblica senese,* cited
supra.

[2] Compare *Il Principe* of Niccolò Machiavelli, edited by L. A. BURD
(Oxford, Clarendon Press, 1891), page 26.

[3] See pages 156-162 of U. G. MONDOLFO'S *Pandolfo Petrucci*
(Siena, tip. Cooperativa, 1899), where the arguments on both sides of
the question are impartially, if succinctly, stated.

the widely different estimates which have been
formed of his character, it is especially regrettable
that the Tavolette which are referable to the period
of his domination have, with one exception, been
destroyed or lost.[1] Unfortunately also that one
remaining Tavoletta throws no light whatever
upon the questions at which I have hinted. Indeed it is not even certain what historical event
it is intended to commemorate. Painted in 1498,
it depicts a group of horsemen entering Siena
by the way of the Camullia Gate. They have
reached the *Antiporto,* and the majority of the
company are opposite the little church of San
Bernardino and the no longer existent Oratory
of San Sepolcro. In the distance is to be seen
the Duomo.

Formerly it was supposed that this picture
was intended to portray the *Entry of Charles VIII.
into Siena,* and, in fact, it is so described in the
Catalogue of 1889; Mr. Berenson, in the index
to his *Central Italian Painters of the Renaissance,*[2]
calls it the " Entrance of Emperor Frederick into
Siena "—an obvious absurdity, in that that event
took place little less than half a century earlier;[3]

[1] Pecci records a Tavoletta di Gabella of 1495, on which was
depicted the construction of a fortress, possibly that of Montepulciano.
It has, however, long since disappeared.

[2] Page 144.

[3] I am perfectly willing to accept Mr. Berenson as a Gamaliel
in matters of art. There he speaks with authority. I must, however, warn the reader that his description of pictures which are " merely

while Luciano Banchi maintains, in an article published in the *Bibliofilo* of March 1880, that it is intended to represent the arrival of an orator of the French King, who, as we learn from the minutes of the *Balìa,*[1] entered Siena in May 1498 and was lodged at the public expense in the Albergo della Corona. This view Signor Lisini appears inclined to adopt as being at least as tenable as any other; and I venture to suggest that, if the following extract from Tommasi's description of the Entry of Charles VIII. does nothing to directly confirm it, it at least completely disposes of the alternative theory:

" At the gate of Camullia, outside the *Antiporto,* in honour of the King was erected a huge triumphal arch, whereupon were two statues, one dedicated to Charlemagne and the other to this same Charles VIII., with certain latin verses which, albeit I have sought for them, I have not been able to find.... Just within the *Antiporto* sat the Signoria with all the Magistrates, the *Antiporto* itself being richly decked. But at the *Porta,* which opens into the city, was a little boy dressed to represent the Mother of God, Lady of the city,

---

illustrative" is not altogether reliable. Witness his statement that the Madonna in the Tavoletta di Biccherna of 1460, who is in fact an aerial presence, is "crowning Pius II." His description of the Tavoletta di Gabella of 1483 as " Four Companies united in Duomo receiving keys", can be attributed only to carelessness in reading the inscription combined with complete ignorance of the meaning of the term *monti.*

[1] *Deliberazioni,* n. 40, c. 154.

who to the sound of many instruments of music
sang these verses with a sweet voice:

Inclyte Francorum Rex invictissime regum
Unica Christicolæ spes, et fiducia gentis
Ingredere, et Felix subeas mea Mœnia, sacris
Auspiciis nam te ipsa libens, vultuque sereno
Urbe mea accipio, felicibus annuo cœptis.
Commictoque tibi Sennonum de nomine Senas."

Is it possible to doubt, in view of the topographical details which distinguish the Tavolette
of this period, that, if the picture under consideration had been intended to represent the entry
of Charles VIII., we should have seen depicted
the *grand'arco trionfale,* and the Magistrates of
the Republic sitting in state?

It only remains to call the attention of the
reader to a lovely Tavoletta di Gabella of 1473,
the work of Sano di Pietro (Plate VII). It represents the marriage in Bologna of Count Roberto Sanseverino, the celebrated condottiere general, with Lucrezia d'Agnolo Malavolti, perhaps
the most beautiful and accomplished lady of her
day. This picture, which was painted, no doubt,
at the suggestion of Misser Agnolo Malavolti, the
father of the bride, who was in that year one of
the Esecutori di Gabella, is full of figures remarkable for elegance of design and freshness of
colour. It amply repays careful study if only for
the light which it throws upon the fashions of
the period.

PLATE VII.

The Tavolette of the XVIth Century.

As Mr. Berenson justly observes, the art of
Siena exhausted itself in presenting the ideals
and feelings of the Middle Ages ; but before the
XVIth century opened the old yearnings ceased
to vex the minds of men and the old ideals failed
to charm. Even Siena could no longer be satisfied
with the few painters who remained to her. Sodoma was summoned from Lombardy, Pinturicchio, Signorelli and Perugino from Umbria and
Fra Paolino from Florence; and "as there were no
forces at home to offer sufficient resistance, there
resulted from all these mingled influences a most
singular and charming eclecticism—saved from
the pretentiousness and folly, usually controlling
such movements, by the sense for grace and beauty
even to the last seldom absent from the Sienese."[1]
This, however, was in the first half of the century.
The fall of the Republic synchronizes very closely
with the death of true art in Siena. What genius
for painting remained when Girolamo del Pacchia
(1477-1535), Domenico Beccafumi (1486-1551)
and Baldassare Peruzzi (1481-1537) had done
their work, was an after-bloom rapidly tending
to decay.

If, however, regarded as works of art, many
of the Tavolette of the XVIth century fall ter-
ribly short of the standard of excellence attained

---

[1] B. BERENSON, *op. cit.*, pages 56, 68.

by those of earlier times, they at least make up
in quantity what they lack in quality. There are
thirty-two of them, and the last Tavole of the
century are measured by feet and yards rather
than by inches. Still, especially at first, some of
them are far from being devoid of merit; while,
regarded as historical documents, they continue
to be of the very first importance until the surrender of Montalcino in 1559.

From the year 1494, when Charles VIII.
crossed the Alps and, instead of encountering a
determined and well-concerted resistance, was
received with an enthusiasm which to himself,
and to his followers alike, appeared unaccount-
able, the fate of the various petty states of Italy
was sealed. Henceforward they were destined to
be used as pawns in the great game played
between France and Spain, and like pawns to
be sacrificed without regret. Thus, during the
XVIth century, the history of each little Prin-
cipality and Commune is no longer of its own
making; and, if we would understand the last
fifty years of the Sienese Republic, we must not
only look beyond the walls of Siena and beyond
her old rivalry with the hated Florence, but even
beyond the bounds of Italy itself. An example
of this condition of things is to be found in the
circumstances which brought about the Battle of
Camullia—the subject of the first Tavoletta which
claims our attention; for it would be worse than

futile to regard that event merely as the result
of the predeliction of a Medicean Pope for that
Sienese faction which had proved itself most
favourable to his House. Rather was it one incident, and that not a specially important incident,
of the war arising out of the " Holy League "
published at Cognac in 1526. Obviously, however, this is no place for the discussion of Eu-
ropean politics, and, for our present purpose, we
may treat the history of Siena as in itself complete.

The Sienese, having expelled the last of the
Petrucci in 1524, placed the Commune under the
protection of the Emperor Charles V. A magistracy was created of " ten conservators of the
liberties of the state; " the different Monti were
united in one named the *Monte de' Nobili Regenti,*
and a new era of freedom was commenced, the
public documents being dated *ab instaurata li-
bertate, anno primo, secundo,* and so forth.·

By this revolution the Noveschi were deprived
of the authority which they had so long enjoyed,
and many of them were driven into exile. They
appealed to Pope Clement VII. for aid, and, in
June 1526, being reinforced by troops from Rome
and Florence, they invaded the Sienese territory
and laid siege to the city ; but the citizens were
prepared for the attack ; as on the eve of Montaperti, they flew to arms, and, like a rain-swollen
river which overflows its banks and carries every-
thing before it, they poured forth from their gates

and swept irresistibly into the hostile camp. There was no discipline among the besiegers and, completely taken by surpise, they broke and fled abandoning their artillery. So sudden and complete was their discomfiture that Vettori declared that the Battle of Camullia appeared to him a fact so extraordinary and portentous that it recalled the victories of the Old Testament when Jehovah himself spread panic-terror among the enemies of his chosen people.[1] Nor were divine manifestations wanting. Warriors clothed in white raiment were seen fighting on behalf of the Sienese: the picture of Our Lady above the great gate of Camullia was illuminated with an unearthly radiance; and, as in 1260, the mantle of the Virgin, in the form of a cloud, spread itself over the city and the combatants.

As I have mentioned elsewhere,[2] a remarkable record of the battle exists in a contemporary painting preserved in the Church of San Martino. There we see the gate with its fortalices, the encampment of the besiegers, bands of soldiers and of citizens, cannons of various and strange forms, huts, banners, and even the female camp-followers, half naked and terrified. For the rest, the im-

---

[1] I have been unable to find this passage in Vettori and quote it on the authority of Professor G. RONDONI, whose *Siena nel secolo XVI* (published in *La vita italiana nel Cinquecento*, Milano, Fratelli Treves, 1897) is as picturesque and powerful a narrative as one would desire to read.

[2] *Our Lady of August and the Palio of Siena* (Siena, E. Torrini, 1899), page 78.

prudence of the Florentines and of their allies
merited no better 'success, and their generals had
no one but themselves to blame if they were held
up to ridicule in the songs which the children
sang about the streets of Siena after the victory;
just as to-day they improvise and sing verses to
celebrate the contest which sends the Palio in
triumph home to their *contrada*.

Quel conton di Pitigliano,
Mangiafichi bufalaio,
Si armò prima col tribbiano,
E poi fece un grand' abbaio.
. . . .
Quel ventron dell'Anguillara
Si fuggì come un poltrone
. . . .
Ci scorgeran per Meucci
Quei Papal Fiorentini ciechi,
Massime Roberto Pucci,
Commessar de' ferri vecchi,
Si fuggì a denti secchi,
Ch' era uscito di memoria,
E narrò la gran vittoria
(pel contrario) a Fiorentini &c.[1]

Such was the Battle of Camullia, the subject
of the Tavoletta di Gabella of 1526, a picture
which well merits attentive study by reason of its
topographical details. It is possibly the work of
the same Giovanni di Lorenzo Cini who executed
the painting in San Martino, above referred to,

---

[1] See the *Memorie storico-critiche della città di Siena* of G. A.
PECCI, part II, page 220.

and who is said to have himself taken part in the fight. Originally, as Alessandro Sozzini informs us,[1] the following legend was inscribed at the foot of the Tavoletta : ROMA SILE IAM FLORENTEM GALLVM VENETVMQ. CLEMENTISQ. LEGAT. PERDOMVISSE DVCES VICTORIA ; but, in 1758, both the inscription and the coats of arms of the Esecutori were erased, and a hideous *barocco* scroll was substituted, bearing the motto which we still see.

In a city like Siena, Ghibelline and Imperial by immemorial tradition, Charles V. naturally acquired an authority which, though nominally exercised only for the protection of the so-called free government, was in fact a thinly disguised absolutism. His counsels were really commands, and he sent his orators to reform the state and to share the government with the magistrates of the Commune. Nor did Siena resent his interference. She gloried in her Emperor as in her strongest and most loyal paladin ; and it was said that her citizens even in their mothers' wombs had upon their lips the name of Cæsar. When, in 1536, Charles visited the city, he was received with almost frenzied joy ; youths of ancient lineage embraced and kissed the legs of his horse, and the highest magistrates of the Republic bowed before him in the dust. Their adulation may have been excessive, but it is hard

------

[1] *Diario*, page 20.

to say that their confidence in his benevolent intentions towards them was misplaced. The Emperor may have meant to keep his word. It was in full accordance with his policy to maintain in the heart of Italy a sincerely friendly state; and, at first, he certainly had no desire to deprive Siena of her liberty. What he demanded of her was that she should set her house in order and that, strong in the union of her citizens and in his support, she should become powerful enough to inspire respect and fear alike in the breasts of the Pope and of the Medici, in neither of whom, thanks to their recent coquetry with France, did he feel able to repose implicit confidence. Unfortunately Siena disregarded his warnings. From 1527 to 1545 the city was torn by faction fights and violent revolts; and, in proportion as the utter incompetence of the Sienese to govern themselves and to live at unity became more and more manifest, the imperial legates and the captains of the Spanish guard assumed an ever increasing authority, until, as time went on, the civic magistrates lost almost every vestige of real power.

Of this epoch we have only one record among the Tavolette; namely that of 1542, which is symbolical of the reforms instituted at the close of the preceding year, at the command of the Emperor by Antoine Perrenot de Granvella Bishop of Arras, whom the Sienese called "Granvela," and Francesco Sfondrato. Here we have a ship wafted towards her haven by one huge bellying

sail, fastened to a leafless tree as to a mast,—
an obvious allusion to the names of the imperial
reformers. On a jagged mass of rocks, near
enough to make the escape of the fortunate mar-
iners appear indeed a narrow one, are to be seen
the shattered remains of another vessel (Plate VIII).

Such was the Tavoletta di Gabella. In the
same year the officials of Biccherna caused a
similar allegory to be painted in commemoration
of the same reforms; and, although this second
Tavoletta no longer exists, we have an adequate
description of it in the *Diario* of Alessandro Sozzini. He says: "It befel that the said Granvela
and Sfondrato were in Siena what time his Catholic Majesty was shipwrecked in Algiers; wherefore the said Granvela was compelled to depart
from the city more quickly than he had intended,
and was unable to finish that which he had begun,
leaving in his stead the said Sfondrato. Now in
that year Girolamo Tommasi was Camarlingo of
Biccherna and he left the *Tavola della sua entrata*
painted upon this wise: a ship on the high seas
with a great sail; in the prow whereof was painted
Justice with scales and a naked sword; on the
poop was painted Granvela who pointed with his
hand toward the harbour, where stood the city
of Siena. At the foot thereof were these verses
written in letters of gold:

TEMPORE DISIECTAM QVO IAM GRANDVELA PER VNDAS,
CÆSARIS ASTREAM REDDIDIT AVSPICIIS. "

PLATE VIII.

QVASSA·M·HANC·SVBOR·CAESA·ÆGVE·AVX··O·NAVE
EX·NAVFRAGIO·AD·MAXIMA···RÉMES·AV·NE·CV
DENVDAT·IA·ARBOR·TVTIORI····VELA·IN·STVRÆ
ERIT·ÆTAER·INSPEXERE·COTIS·HIRVDINA·CNRL·K
M·D····

— 89 —

We ask ourselves whether this allegory was
the result of mere servile adulation or rather the
embodiment of a patriotic yearning for better
things.[1] Possibly the sentiments to which it owed
its birth were not unmixed for Siena still trusted
her Cæsar.

Of all the ministers whom Charles sent to
Siena the wisest were Granvela and Sfondrato,
the worst Don Giovanni de Luna and Don Diego
Hurtado de Mendoza, that

> Arcimarrano
> Nemico a tutta Italia, al ciel e al mondo,

who, as the Mangia wrote to Riccio the painter,
possessed

> il viso ursegno
> D'un moro bianco, con l'occhio porcino ;
> Cera proprio di furbo e d'assassino,[2]

and whose *tanti falli*, in the opinion of another
Sienese poet, merited no less a punishment than

> La forcha, 'l fuoco, 'l carro e la tanaglia.[3]

---

[1] That the Sienese really believed that this reform had been ef-
fectual for good seems reasonably clear from the letter written by the
magistrates of the Republic to Fra Bernardino Ochino in 1542. A translation will be found in KARL BENRATH's *Bernardino Ochino of Siena*
(London, 1876), page 95.

[2] A. SOZZINI, *Diario* (Firenze, Vieusseux, 1842), Document XIV,
page 456. *Sonetto, che manda il* MANGIA *della Torre del Campo a maestro* RICCIO *Pittore a Pisa per far ritrarre Don* DIEGO *di Mendozza*.

[3] *Sonetto contro Don Diego Urtado da Mendozza* published in
the *Miscellanea storica senese,* vol. V (1898), pages 176-7.

No doubt these views are not impartial, and we might as reasonably expect to form a just estimate of Lord Milner's work in South Africa from the statements of the pro Boer press as to obtain an unbiassed idea of Don Diego's merits and demerits from contemporary Sienese writers. Nevertheless the fact remains that the government of the author of the " History of the War of Granada " destroyed all the old confidence of Siena in the benevolent intentions of her Emperor. Love was turned to hatred,[1] and patient submission to furious revolt. In July 1552 the Spanish garrison was expelled and the fortress which Don Diego had erected to overawe the city was razed to the ground. This victory was celebrated on the Tavolette both of Biccherna and of Gabella. There we see the work of demolition painted by a contemporary artist (both the Tavolette are attributed to Giorgio di Giovanni) who had probably himself taken part in that festival of destruction. Magistrates, priests, nobles and artisans, even little children (*citti e citte*) laboured with such good will that, in one short hour, *ne fu guasta tanta verso la città, che non se ne saria murata in quattro mesi.*[2] Thus did Our Lady

---

[1] Compare *Il Pater noster della Repubblica di Siena* published in the *Miscellanea storica senese*, vol. III (1895), page 178. The first verse runs:

Ecco che pur da le rapaci mani
Di Carlo Quinto, 'l più Tiranno e rio
N' hai liberati e dai spagnol marani,
Pater Noster.

[2] Sozzini, *Diario*, page 90.

vindicate her honour and bring to naught the scornful boast of Don Diego that he would present upon her altar the keys of his fortress; and therefore is she depicted in each of the Tavolette as superintending its overthrow.

No sooner had the Spaniards departed than, with characteristic frivolity (Dante's epithet of "gente vana" was not altogether a slander), the good Sienese gave themselves up to enjoyment; and "they passed two months in gaiety without ever speaking of war, thinking only of fowling, hunting and making merry"[1]—and this although, with the exception of Buonconvento, Montalcino and Monteriggioni, almost all the fortresses and walled places of the contado were in a state of disrepair. In some the walls were ruinous; in some the gates were off their hinges; water penetrated into the casemates and many of the cannons were so rusted as to be unworkable.[2]

In December the awakening came. News was brought that the Emperor "was levying horse and foot in the Kingdom of Naples to come to the damage of the city of Siena and of its Dominion." At the beginning of February the invading army spread over Valdichiana; Lucignano and Montefollonico surrendered without resistance; San Quirico was abandoned, and, although Monticchiello held out gallantly for more than two weeks, the

---

[1] Sozzini, *Diario*, page 92.
[2] See Falletti-Fossati, *op. cit.*, and compare the Milanesi *Documents*, III, 115-117.

garrison "were compelled to defend themselves
with stones, since powder was lacking for the
arquebuses."[1] Their resistance, however, gave
Montalcino a little breathing space in which to
prepare to meet the coming storm; and, short
as it was, it proved sufficient. Men and women
laboured day and night on the fortifications, and
for two months and eighteen days the imperialists
bombarded her walls in vain, until, in the middle
of June 1553, they were compelled to raise the
siege and hurry southward to resist a threatened
invasion of the Turks.

The Tavoletta di Biccherna of this year represents the city of Montalcino besieged by the
imperialists, with a delineation of the entrenchments
and of the offensive and defensive works. An assault
is being made by the besiegers. The scene with
all its details is one of quite exceptional interest,
since it seems almost certain that we may attribute it to Giorgio di Giovanni, architect and painter, to whom had been entrusted the construction
of the defensive works which he here depicts.[2]

Montalcino had beaten off her foes and Siena
rejoiced but for the last time. Her day was al-

---

[1] AMMIRATO, *Istorie Fiorentine* (edition cited), tom. VI, page 318.
[2] The MILANESI *Documents*, III, 197-200, 206 : see also *Il campo imperiale sotto Montalcino nel 1553, narrazione storica di Anonimo contemporaneo*, edited by L. BANCHI and A. LISINI, Siena, Gati, 1885.— A reproduction of this Tavoletta is there published and on pages XII-XIV the arguments are adduced which render it probable that it was painted by Giorgio di Giovanni.

most done. She had had her splendid morning, her long changeful afternoon, her stormy evening; and now her sun was about to set in such a blaze of glory that perhaps the world shall never see the like again.

Of the last great siege I shall not speak. That story of splendid hopeless courage, of unavailing self-sacrifice, of fiendish cruelty, of squalid suffering, is known to all who know the name Siena. Enough in this place to call attention to the last Tavoletta of the free Commune, painted in 1555. There the Apostle Paul, a tall imposing figure, points with his right hand to the legend inscribed beneath his feet: OMNES QVI VOLVNT IVSTE VIVERE PERSECVTIONEM PATIVNTVR. Behind him, fair and many towered, lies Siena; and perhaps we may believe that he wishes to console her with the thought that, even as persecutions came upon him and the Lord delivered him out of them all, so may she yet be delivered.[1]

When on the 21st April the Spanish troops entered the city, two hundred and forty-two nobles and four hundred and thirty-five *popolani* departed with their families to take refuge in Montalcino, where, for four years, they maintained a shadowy form of republic; nor was it until their last hope of succour was destroyed by the peace of Cateau Cambrésis, whereby the French claims

---

[1] See 2 *Timothy* III, 11, 12. – The inscription of the Tavoletta is an adaptation of verse 12. *Et omnes qui pie volunt vivere in Christo Jesu persecutionem patientur.*

were abandoned and the Spanish hegemony was
formally acknowledged, that they finally yielded
to the inevitable.

In a Tavola di Biccherna of 1558 we see for
the first time the Medicean arms, with the motto
SEMPER. Above stands the Madonna surrounded
by cherubs, her hands extended as if to bless,
being thus transformed into a sort of celestial
' Vicar of Bray ' prepared to side with the winner
even though he might be a Florentine Grand Duke
trampling beneath his feet the liberties of her
faithful city.

The Tavola di Biccherna of 1559 records the
Peace of Cateau Cambrésis. There Henry of
France and Philip of Spain are depicted beneath
a portico in the act of embracing. On either side
stand many courtiers and soldiers. In the distance
are to be seen Siena and Montalcino. The Tavola of Gabella of the same year represents the
delivery of the keys of the latter city to the agents
of Philip II. Round about its border we read the
following legend: LIBERA SENENSIS RESPVBLICA
CESSIT IN VRBEM ILCINEI MONTIS, CLAVESQVE
HINC DETVLIT VLTRO IMPERIVMQVE DVCI COSMO
CVI SIDERA SVMMA INGENS PROMICTVNT SCEP-
TRVM MAIORAQVE REGNA.

By the patent of investiture of 1557 Cosimo
de' Medici had become master of Siena and of
her dominion. His solemn entry into the city is
depicted in a Tavola of 1561—a very mean picture, but curious in its details.

Henceforward the principal scope of the Ta-
volette is to illustrate the annals of the House of
Medici—baptisms, marriages, coronations. It suf-
fices thus to have mentioned them. With the
Tavolette of 1559 the series, regarded as a Pic-
torial Chronicle of the Republic, comes to an end.
Spain and the Papacy had quenched for three
centuries the genial light of Italy. The Catholic
Reaction swept away scholarship, poetry, paint-
ing, sculpture, architecture and free thought. For
Siena, as for the whole Peninsula, the words of
Michael Angelo's Night were fittest :—

'Tis sweet to sleep, sweeter of stone to be,
  And while endure the infamy and woe,
For me 'tis happiness not to feel or see.
  Do not awake me therefore. Ah, speak low!

Of the remaining Tavolette there is but little
to be said. Scarcely one of them has any decorative value, and, if we regard them merely as illustrations, the fact that they illustrate a period which
most lovers of Italy would willingly forget, does
not add to our enjoyment of them.

With the fall of the Republic the existence of
Siena as part of a modern state began ; and, as
a necessary consequence, her political horizon was
enlarged ; for it is obvious that each state must
feel a certain interest in the doings of other states,
and for good or ill must itself be influenced to a
more or less appreciable extent by the fortunes of
its neighbours. Thus it is that events of Euro-

pean importance always find an echo in the talk of
the city, in the columns of the local papers, in
poetry whether literary or popular, in the books
and pictures of the period ; and thus, in the
XVIth century, the history of other nations began
to find a place in the Tavole of Biccherna and
of Gabella.

The commemoration in the Tavolette of the
Peace of Cateau Cambrésis may, of course, be
accounted for by the very definite consequences
which that reconciliation had for the state of
Siena. However, as early as 1533, a Tavola di
Biccherna records the victory of Andrea Doria
over the Turkish fleet in the Gulf of Messinia,
while immediately after the fall ot the Republic
no fewer than three Tavolette are referable to the
war against the Infidels.

During the XVIth century the Turks were a
constant menace to Christendom, and it has been
truly said that the enslavement of Italy by Spain
probably saved her from a relapse into barbarism
under Mahommedan conquerors. In the eight
years of Selim's reign (1512-1520) the Ottoman
empire had been almost doubled in extent. His
son Suleyman drove the knights of St. John from
Rhodes, while to the northward his armies swept
round the walls of Vienna. Barbarossa won Algiers for Turkey and held the Mediterranean
against the fleets of Spain and Italy : Torghud
added Tripoli to the empire : and Piyála routed
the galleys of Genoa, Naples and Sicily off the

Island of Jerba. This was in 1560; and well might Italy tremble before

> ..... il Turco crudel che d'ora in ora
> Per la discordia de' principi adopra
> Sempre a mio danno e quasi mi divora.

In 1565 the Infidels once more measured swords with the knights of St. John who had taken refuge in Malta. On May 18th the Turkish fleet under the redoubtable Dragut appeared in sight, and one of the most celebrated sieges in history began. It was finally raised on the 8th of September after the death of Dragut and twenty-five thousand of his followers. On the scene of this desperate struggle subsequently rose the city of Valetta. The victory is depicted in a Tavola di Biccherna of 1566. In 1570 we find a representation of the *League of Venice* which, however, did not avail to prevent the slaughter of Famagosta and the cruel death of the heroic Marcantonio Bragadino. In 1571 we have the *Battle of Lepanto,* in which the Turkish fleet was almost annihilated—a success which was potent in fanning the flame of Catholic enthusiasm.

The Tavola di Biccherna of 1582, which is commemorative of the *Reform of the Calendar,* deserves to be described at somewhat greater length, not only because it is of higher merit than most of the pictures belonging to a period

7

during which, in the words of Mr. Symonds,[1] " art sank into a slough of slovenly and soulless putrescence," but also by reason of the interest which it possesses as an historical curiosity.

In the year 325 A. D., it being considered desirable to establish precisely the period of the celebration of Easter according to the Christian traditions, and with reference to the spring equinox and the full moon, the Council of Nicæa agreed that, to obviate the effects of certain errors of computation in the Julian Calendar, which was the one then in use, the spring equinox, which had been placed therein on the 25th of March, should be put back to the 21st of that month. The Council, having fixed that date, did not go into the matter any further ; and, the errors of the Calendar not having been corrected, the equinox continued to retrocede, and the difference between the astronomical and the ecclesiastical year became annually greater.

This ever increasing discrepancy began to be obvious to all thinking persons in the first centuries of the Middle Ages, and because it brought about, or at any rate, would have brought about in time, difficulties with regard to the ecclesiastical liturgy and inevitable conflict between the traditional authority of Holy Church on the one hand and the laws of science on the other, the matter commenced to be seriously discussed, and

---

[1] *Renaissance in Italy. The Catholic Reaction* (London, Smith Elder & Co., 1898), part II, page 209.

occupied the minds of illustrious mathematicians and astronomers, such as Johannes de Sacro Bosco (John Holywood), Roger Bacon, Nicolaus Cusanus, and Regiomontanus (Johann Müller). The Councils of the Church and the Universities debated the matter, mixing up questions ecclesiastical and astronomical, political and commercial. The advocates of a reform of the Calendar were alternately favoured and rebuked; but finally a Commission of learned men of divers nationalities assembled in the Vatican at the call of Pope Gregory XIII., and, opinions having been gathered from all parts of Christendom, the plan of reform proposed by Aloysius Lilius (Luigi Lilio Ghiraldi), a learned Calabrian astronomer and physician, was approved. The Pope proclaimed the reform in the Bull *Inter gravissimas* on the 24th day of February 1582. Owing, however, to the divergence of religious views and political interests, the *Gregorian Calendar* or *New Style* did not immediately obtain adhesion throughout the whole of Christendom; but in the greater part of the Catholic States it was adopted at once; and, as far as Tuscany is concerned, it is enough to mention that the proclamation in reference to the reform was published by the order of the Grand Duke Francesco I. dei Medici, in Florence on the 20th June 1582 and in Siena on the 10th of July of the same year. Scipione di Crescenzio Turamini, Camarlingo di Biccherna, was then finishing his term of office, and of this

great fact of the Gregorian reform, which hap-
pened during his official life, he has preserved
for us a record in the Tavola above mentioned.

To the left of the picture is the Pope, seated
upon a throne surmounted by a canopy. He
holds in his left hand a scroll—possibly the re-
port of the Commission or a draft of the Bull of
Reform—while he raises the finger of his right
hand as if to bespeak attention. On either side
of the throne stand cardinals and minor ecclesiastics
as also a halberdier. Through an open archway
a full light falls upon the Pontiff. Before him,
seated at a long table covered with green cloth,
are seen cardinals, bishops, friars and doctors.
Some of these have turned towards the Pope,
some are disputing with one another, others make
computations on their fingers. In the midst of
them stands a prelate with a long staff which he
holds in his right hand, and with which he points
to certain signs of the zodiac which are painted
in a frame hung upon the wall. In his left hand,
which is resting upon a globe, he holds a pair
of compasses. This is evidently one of the principal members of the Commission, but we have no
means of ascertaining whether or no it is an actual
portrait. We should like to see what manner of
man Antonio Lilio Ghiraldi, who carried out the
plan of reform of his dead brother Luigi, was;
or to recognize in this figure the Cardinal Guglielmo Sirleto who, himself a Calabrian, doubtless did much to promote the scheme proposed

by his fellow countryman; but the costume is not that of either a cardinal or a doctor.

However, this, after all, is a minor matter. The importance of the Tavola does not depend upon the accuracy with which the persons and things which it represents are delineated, but rather on the fact that it records a scientific event of world-wide influence, and testifies, in the midst of much degeneracy, to a culture which could find an interest and an expansion beyond the walls of Siena and beyond the confines of the State. Moreover it is to be observed that some years before, when Gregory had sent round a draft of the proposed Lilian Reform to obtain the opinion of the learned in regard to it, among the numerous Italians who forwarded authoritative opinions, there were not lacking two Sienese: Alessandro Piccolomini, Bishop of Patrasso, and Teofilo Marzio, a Cassinese monk.[1]

A Tavola di Biccherna of 1585, which represents a skirmish between the troops of Pope Sixtus V. and the brigands of the Roman Campagna, is interesting because, in the right hand corner, we see the Basilica of St. Peter and in the foreground the great obelisk which had then been newly placed in the position which it still occupies. Two Tavole of the XVIIth century contain views of the Piazza del Campo, and there

---

[1] See C. PAOLI, *Le Tavolette dipinte*, &c., *op. cit.*, pages 22-24.

are several which refer to the Madonna of Provenzano and the construction of her church—an event which I have discussed so fully in another place that it can hardly be necessary to allude to it again.[1]

And now, before taking leave of the Tavolette, I would ask the reader to consider for a moment the last fifteen or twenty of them—those of the XVIth century—merely with regard to their colour. Where now is the gold and the blue, *le figure adornate e lavorate d' azzuro fino oltremarino e oro,* and the *altri fini colori,* which appealed so strongly to the old Sienese, and of which the painters of an earlier date made such lavish use?[2] A return to the first room and a second glance at Sano di Pietro's *Marriage of Lucrezia Malavolti* will serve to emphasize the contrast. And the change has been a very sudden one. The Republic puts itself under Spanish protection, and lo ! in an instant, almost as it were by the waving of a magician's wand,

. . . . there hath past away a glory from the earth.

When Charles V. entered Siena in April 1536, he was clad, as a contemporary writer informs us, " with great simplicity, to wit in a black velvet

---

[1] *Our Lady of August and the Palio of Siena,* chap. V.
[2] See the MILANESI *Documents,* vol. II, pages 256-258.

doublet, while upon his head was a brocaded cap of black silk without any other ornament; about his neck was a golden collar wherefrom hung an *Agnus Dei* also of gold and of no great weight." [1] He had worn the same sombre garments at Bologna five years earlier; and, in a short space of time, it became the fashion throughout Italy to adopt the subdued tone of Spanish clothing. "The upper classes," says Mr. Symonds, [2] "consented to exchange the varied and brilliant dresses which gave gaiety to the earlier Renaissance for the dismal severity conspicuous in Morone's masterpieces, in the magnificent gloom of the Genoese Brignoli, and in the portraits of the Roman Inquisitors. It is as if the whole race had put on mourning for its loss of liberty, its servitude to foreign tyrants and ecclesiastical hypocrites. Nor is it fanciful to detect a note of moral sadness and mental depression corresponding to these black garments in the faces of that later generation. How different is Tasso's melancholy grace from Ariosto's gentle joyousness; the dried-up precision of Baroccio's Francesco Maria della Rovere from the sanguine joviality of Titian's first duke of that name! One of the most acutely critical of contemporary poets felt the change which I have in-

---

[1] *Carlo Quinto in Siena nell'Aprile del 1536 ; relazione di un contemporaneo pubblicata per cura di* PIETRO VIGO (Bologna, Gaetano Romagnoli, 1884), page 26.

[2] *Op. cit.,* pages 33-34.

dicated, and ascribed it to the same cause. Campanella wrote as follows:

Black robes befit our age.   Once they were white;
Next many-hued; now dark as Afric's Moor,
Night-black, infernal, traitorous, obscure,
Horrid with ignorance and sick with fright.
For very shame we shun all colours bright,
Who mourn our end—the tyrants we endure,
The chains, the noose, the lead, the snares, the lure—
Our dismal heroes, our souls sunk in night."

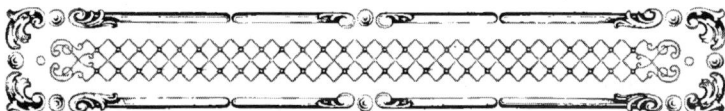

LIST OF *TAVOLETTE DIPINTE DELLA BICCHERNA E DELLA GABELLA* CONTAINED IN THE SIENESE ARCHIVES.

NOTE.

The following list does not purport to include all existent Tavolette, but only such of them as are represented in the *Archivio di Stato in Siena*. Where the titles of the pictures are printed' in ordinary type the originals are in the Sienese collection; where italics are used only photographs (or, in one case, a facsimile) will be found there.

The author is alone responsible for the attributions although he is glad to acknowledge his indebtedness to the works of Signor Lisini and of Mr. Berenson, and to the kind assistance and advice of Professor Langton–Douglas.

Should the dates given in this list occasionally seem to be at variance with those inscribed upon the Tavolette, the explanation may be found in the fact that the modern system of computation is here adopted, whereas the Sienese year began on the 25th of March.

The numerals which follow the titles of the various pictures denote the pages on which the same are referred to in the present work.

1258. BICCHERNA.
Don Ugo, Monk of San Galgano, Camarlingo,
Gilio di Pietro .... 23 n., 33, 38

1263. BICCHERNA.
Coats of Arms of the four Provveditori,
Unknown .... 23 n., 33

1264. BICCHERNA.
Ildebrandino Pagliaresi, Camarlingo, **Dieti=
salvi** .... 23 n.

1267. BICCHERNA.
Coats of Arms of the four Provveditori, **Die=
tisalvi** .... 23 n.

1270. BICCHERNA ....
Ranieri Pagliaresi, Camarlingo, **Dietisalvi**. 32-33

1273. BICCHERNA.
Coats of Arms of the four Provveditori, **Un=
known** 32-33

(NOTE.—In the lower half of the Tavoletta is depicted the Potestà in
act of passing judgment on a criminal. This is, however, a compara-
tively modern addition.)

1276. BICCHERNA.
Don Bartolomeo, Monk of San Galgano, Camarlingo, **Unknown** 32-33

1280. BICCHERNA.
Don Guido, Monk of San Galgano, Camarlingo, **Guido** .... 23 n.

1291. GABELLA.
Coats of Arms of the three Esecutori, **Mas=
saruccio** .... 32-33, 34 n.

1307. GABELLA.
Coats of Arms of the three Esecutori, together
with the portrait of Fra Masino degli Umiliati, Camarlingo, **Unknown** .... 34 n.

1314. BICCHERNA.
To the left, Fra Jacomo degli Umiliati, Camarlingo, together with the Arms of the
Potestà, Carlo del Conte Guido da Battifolle. *To the right*, the arms of the Provveditori, **Unknown** 34

(NOTE. — In subsequent Tavolette the same arrangement will be
found to exist with regard to the portrait of the Camarlingo, the Arms
of the Potestà and those of the Quattro Provveditori. In future, in
such cases, I shall economize space by merely giving the name of the
Camarlingo.)

1320. BICCHERNA.
San Galgano, **Guido Cinatti** (?) 39, 44

1324. BICCHERNA.
Don Gregorio degli Umiliati, Camarlingo,
Unknown.

1329. BICCHERNA.
*Don Niccolò, Monk of San Galgano, Camar-
lingo*, **Unknown**.

1334. GABELLA.
The Nativity, **Unknown** ... . 34 n., 39, 40

1344. GABELLA.
Allegory of Good Government, **Ambrogio.
Lorenzetti** 40, 44-47, 57

1353. BICCHERNA.
The Camarlingo and Scrittore di Biccherna,
Bartolomeo Bulgarini.

1357. GABELLA.
The Circumcision of Christ, **School of Ambrogio Lorenzetti**.................. 39

1367. BICCHERNA.
The Holy Trinity, with attendant Saints,
Unknown 39

1385. BICCHERNA.
Allegory of the Government of Siena, **School
of Lorenzetti**.................. 40, 45-50, 57

1388. BICCHERNA.
The Camarlingo and Scrittore, **Unknown.**

1389. BICCHERNA.
The Camarlingo and Scrittore, **Unknown.**

1393. BICCHERNA.
The Camarlingo and Scrittore, **Unknown.** 39

1394. BICCHERNA.
The Camarlingo and Scrittore, **Unknown.** 39

1433. BICCHERNA.
Coronation of the Emperor Sigismund, **Unknown** 66

1436. BICCHERNA.
St. Jerome in the desert, **School of Giovanni di Paolo** 56

1437. BICCHERNA.
Allegory of the Pestilence, **School of Giovanni di Paolo** 58-60

1440. GABELLA.
S. Pietro Alessandrino, **Giovanni di Paolo.** 56

1444. GABELLA
St. Michael the Archangel, **Giovanni di Paolo** 56

1445. GABELLA.
The Annunciation, **Manner of Giovanni di Paolo** 56

1449 BICCHERNA.
Coronation of Pope Nicolas V., **Unknown**. 67-68

1451. BICCHERNA.
Ghino di Pietro Bellanti, Camarlingo, **Unknown** 61

1455. GABELLA.
The Annunciation, **Unknown** 69

1457. BICCHERNA.
Allegorical Picture, **Sano di Pietro** 70

1460. BICCHERNA.
Coronation of Pope Pius II., **Lorenzo di Pietro** (? . . . . 70-71, 79 n.

1460 GABELLA.
Pius II. investing his nephew with the Cardinal's hat, **Francesco di Giorgio Martini** 70

1467. BICCHERNA.
The Madonna protecting Siena in the time of Earthquakes, **Francesco di Giorgio Martini** 61-64

1468. GABELLA
Allegory of Peace and War, **Unknown** . . . 60-61

1471. GABELLA.
The Wisdom which proceeds from God, **Sano di Pietro** 56

1473. GABELLA.
Marriage of Madonna Lucrezia Malavolti, **Sano di Pietro** 80,102

1474. GABELLA.
Allegory of the Government of Siena, **School of Benvenuto di Giovanni** 56-57

1479. GABELLA.
Allied forces entering Colle di Val d' Elsa, **Francesco di Giorgio Martini** 71-73

1480. GABELLA.
The Virgin recommending the City of Siena to Christ, **Francesco di Giorgio Martini** 73-74

1483. GABELLA.
Presentation of the Keys of Siena to the Virgin, **Unknown** .... 74, 79 n.

1484. GABELLA.
The Virgin presented in the Temple, **Guidoccio Cozzarelli** 56

1485. GABELLA.
The Sacrifice of Isaac, **Guidoccio Cozzarelli** 75

1487. GABELLA.
Allegorical Picture — The Madonna guiding into port the Sienese Ship of State, **Bernardino Fungai** 75

1489. GABELLA.
The Camarlingo and Esecutori beseeching the Virgin and Child to enter Siena, **Un= known** 64–65

1498. BICCHERNA.
Horsemen entering the *Antiporto* of Camullia, **Unknown** 78–80

1499. GABELLA.
St. Catherine receiving the stigmata, **Man= ner of Guidoccio Cozzarelli** 70

1523. BICCHERNA.
Christ, St. Thomas and St. Bartholomew, **Unknown**.

1526. GABELLA.
Battle of Camullia, **Giovanni di Lorenzo Cini** 82–86

1528. GABELLA.
Below, Christ taking the heart of St. Cather-ine. *Above*, Christ offering his heart to her, **Unknown**.

1533. BICCHERNA.
Victory of Andrea Doria over the Turkish fleet, **Unknown**...................... 96

1534. BICCHERNA.
Coronation of Pope Paul III., **Unknown**.

1539. GABELLA.
Espousal of St. Catherine, **Unknown**.

1542. GABELLA.
Allegory of the reforms instituted by Gran-vela and Sfondrato, **Unknown**........ 87-88

1546. BICCHERNA.
Crucifixion, **School of Beccafumi**.

1548. BICCHERNA.
Virgin and Child with the two St. Catherines,
Domenico Beccafumi (?).

1552. BICCHERNA.
Demolition of Spanish fortress, **Giorgio di
Giovanni** 90-91

1552. GABELLA.
Demolition of Spanish fortress, **Giorgio di
Giovanni**........................ 90-91

1553. BICCHERNA.
Siege of Montalcino, **Giorgio di Giovanni.** 92

1555. GABELLA.
St. Paul with the City of Siena in the back-
ground, **Giorgio di Giovanni**........ 93

1558. BICCHERNA.
Above, The Madonna surrounded by cherubs.
Below, The Medicean arms with the motto
SEMPER, **Unknown** ....,.......... 94

1559. BICCHERNA.
The Peace of Cateau Cambrésis, **Giorgio
di Giovanni** 94, 96

1559. GABELLA.
Surrender of Montalcino, **Giorgio di Giovanni** 94, 95

1560-1. BICCHERNA.
Cosimo dei Medici receiving the insignia of
Grand Master of the Order of St. Stephen

at the hands of the Papal legate, **Un=
known**.

1561. BICCHERNA.
Entry of Duke Cosimo I. into Siena, **Un=
known**.. 94

1566. BICCHERNA.
Defeat of the Turks at Malta, **Unknown**. 97

1567. BICCHERNA.
The seven fat kine of Pharaoh's vision with
Bacchus and Ceres, **Unknown**.

(NOTE. — The Allegory is explained by the inscription.)

1568-9. BICCHERNA.
The Battle of Lepanto, **Unknown** 97

(NOTE.— The inscription on this Tavola runs AL TEMPO DI NIC-
COLÒ DI CORNELIO BORGHESI KAMARLINGO DI BICCHERNA 1568; but,
since the Battle of Lepanto was not fought until 7 October 1571, it
is clear that he caused it to be painted some time after his term of
office had expired.)

1570-1. BICCHERNA.
The Ambassadors of Philip II. and Republic
of Venice enter into a league with Pope
Pius V. against the Turks, **Unknown**.. 97

1574-5. BICCHERNA.
Virgin and Child with St. Catherine of Siena
and St. John the Baptist.—The kneeling
figure is Cav. Alamanno Marescotti, Camarlingo, **Manner of Beccafumi**.

1575-6. BICCHERNA.
The Annunciation, **School of Beccafumi**.

1582-83. BICCHERNA.
The Reform of the Calendar, **Unknown** .. 97-101

1585-6. BICCHERNA.
Skirmish between Papal troops and Brigands,
Unknown 101

1586-87. BICCHERNA.
Holy Trinity, **Unknown**.

1587-8. BICCHERNA.
Sienese Ambassadors do homage to Cardinal
Ferdinando de' Medici, Grand Duke of
Tuscany, **Antonio Gregori**.

1588-9. BICCHERNA.
Wedding of Ferdinando I. de' Medici with
Cristina daughter of Charles of Lorraine,
Ventura Salimbeni.

1589-90. BICCHERNA.
Baptism of Cosimo II. de' Medici, **Ventura
Salimbeni**.

1592-4. BICCHERNA.
The Officials of the Concistoro and of the
Balìa of Siena venerate the Madonna of
Provenzano, **Unknown** 102

1595-8. BICCHERNA.
Entrance of Clement VIII. into Ferrara, **Un=
known**.

1601-4. BICCHERNA.
The Madonna of Provenzano, St. Catherine
and San Bernardino, **Francesco Vanni**. 102

1605-6. BICCHERNA.
Pope Paul V. promotes his cousin and name-
sake Camillo Borghesi, Bishop of Montalcino, to the Archbishopric of Siena, **Ven=
tura Salimbeni**.

1608. GABELLA.
The Madonna of Provenzano, St. Catherine
and San Bernardino, **Unknown** 102

1608-10. BICCHERNA.
Tournament in the Piazza del Campo, **Un=
known** 101

1610. GABELLA.
Return of the Compagnia di San Bernardino
from a pilgrimage to the City of Aquila,
Unknown 101

(NOTE. — The Tavola is more fully explained by its inscription.)

1610-13. BICCHERNA.
The Madonna of Provenzano carried in procession to the Church which still bears her
name, **Manner of Ventura Salimbeni**. 102

1619. BICCHERNA.
San Carlo Borromeo, **Francesco Rustici**.

1677-82. BICCHERNA.
San Galgano, **Unknown** 44

CHRONOLOGICAL TABLE

OF THE

PRINCIPAL SIENESE PAINTERS.

———

GUIDO DA SIENA, flourished in 1221.

GILIO DI PIETRO, painted a Tavoletta di Biccherna in 1258.

DIETISALVI PETRONI, flourished between 1259 and 1282.

VENTURA DI GUALTIERI, of whom we have record in 1264 and 1270.

GUIDO DI GRAZIANO, died early in the XIVth century.

MASSARUCCIO, painted a Tavoletta di Gabella in 1291.

DUCCIO DI BUONINSEGNA, born about 1260; died 1340.

SEGNA DI BUONAVENTURA DI BUONINSEGNA, flourished in 1305.

PIETRO LORENZETTI, first recorded in 1305; probably died in the great pestilence of 1348.

AMBROGIO LORENZETTI, born at the close of the XIIIth century; died about 1348.

SIMONE MARTINI, born 1285? died 1344.

LIPPO MEMMI, died 1357.

LIPPO DI VANNI, still living in March 1375.

GIACOMO DI MINO DEL PELLICCIAIO, flourished in 1342; was dead in 1396.

BARTOLO DI MAESTRO FREDI, born 1330?; died 1410.

LUCA DI TOMMÈ, flourished in 1355; died 1381.

BERNA, flourished in 1370; died 1381?.

PAOLO DI GIOVANNI, flourished in 1381.

ANDREA DI VANNI, born about 1332; died about 1414.

TADDEO DI BARTOLO, born 1363; died 1422.

SANO DI PIETRO, born 1406; died 1481.

DOMENICO DI BARTOLO, died about 1449.

GIOVANNI DI PAOLO, inscribed on the roll of painters in 1428; died 1482?.

LORENZO DI PIETRO (il VECCHIETTA), born 1410; died 1480.

STEFANO DI GIOVANNI (SASSETTA), died 1450.

MATTEO DI GIOVANNI BARTOLI, born 1420; died 1495.

BENVENUTO DI GIOVANNI, born 1436; died about 1518.

NEROCCIO DI BARTOLOMMEO LANDI, born 1447; died 1500.

FRANCESCO DI GIORGIO MARTINI, born 1439; died 1502.

GUIDOCCIO COZZARELLI, born 1450; died 1516.

BERNARDINO FUNGAI, born 1460; died 1516.

ANTONIO BARILI, born 1453; died 1516.

ANDREA DI NICCOLÒ, born 1460; died 1529.

GIROLAMO DI BENVENUTO, born 1470; died 1524.

GIACOMO PACCHIAROTTI, born 1474; died about 1540.

GIROLAMO DEL PACCHIA, born 1477; died 1535.

GIOVANNI DI LORENZO CINI, still living in 1538.

BALDASSARE PERUZZI, born 1481; died 1537.

DOMENICO BECCAFUMI, born 1486 ; died 1551.

GIORGIO DI GIOVANNI, died 1559?.

LORENZO RUSTICI, born 1512 ; died 1572.

BARTOLOMMEO NERONI (il RICCIO) ; died 1571.

ARCANGIOLO SALIMBENI, died 1580.

ALESSANDRO CASOLANI, born 1541 ; died 1607.

PIETRO SORRI, born 1556 ; died 1622.

VENTURA SALIMBENI (son of ARCANGIOLO), born 1557 ; died 1613.

FRANCESCO VANNI, born 1563 ; died 1610.

FRANCESCO RUSTICI or RUSTICHINO, died 1626.

RUTILIO DI LORENZO MANETTI, born 1572 ; died 1639.

ASTOLFO PETRAZZI, born 1579 ; died 1653.

INDEX.

ADVOCATA *Senensium*, 61, 64, 65.
Agazzari, Fra Filippo, 59.
Aggregati, The, 73.
Alessandrino, The Blessed Pietro, 35, 56 n.
Alfonso, Duke of Calabria, 73.
Algiers, 88, 96.
Allegorical Tavolette, 44, 56 seq.
Ambasciata cum uno equo, 21 n.
Ambrogio Lorenzetti : see *Lorenzetti Ambrogio*.
Andrea Doria, 96.
Angiolieri Cecco, 22.
Anguillara, 85.
Armouries, State, under the superintendence of the
    Provveditori, 27.
Art, Conservatism of Sienese, 51 seq.
Arte degli Speziali, 56 n.
Arte della Lana, 46 n.
Arte de' Pittori, 42, 52.
Artisans, Banishment of four thousand, 47.

BACKGAMMON: see *Tavole, Game of*.
Bacon Roger, 99.
Baldassare Peruzzi, 51, 81.
Balìa, Il Magnifico Collegio della, 44, 79.

Balie, 16.

Balzana, The, 57 n., 70, 71.

Banco, 32.

Banditori, 27.

Bankers, 46 n.

Barattiere, 59.

Barbarinus custos Biccherne, 23 n.

Barbarossa, 96.

Baths of the Sienese contado, 30.

Beccafumi Domenico, 51, 81.

Bellanti Ghino di Pietro, 61.

Belle Arti, Pictures in the Galleria delle, 36, 57 n., 70.

Benedict, Rule of St., 18.

Benvenuto di Giovanni, 53, 57, 60.

Berenson, Mr., quoted 42 n., 81; his depreciation of
the work of Ambrogio Lorenzetti, 45 n.; his inac-
curate description of pictures, 78-79 n.

Bernardino, San; denounces the election of ecclesiastical
Camarlinghi, 19 n.

Bernard of Clairvaux, St., 69.

Berrovieri, 20.

Bianco da Siena, 55 n.

Biccherna: derivation of the word, 17; office of, when
formed, 17; where situated, 17; internal arrangements of, 39; pictures painted on the walls of, 35, 36,
71; officials of, 18 seq.; Books of, 21 seq.; Power
of, curtailed by Cosimo de' Medici, 28; abolished by
Pietro Leopoldo, 17.

Blessed Damozel, D. G. Rossetti's, 55 n.

Bonicus Bonici castaldus comunis, 21 n.

Boni homines, 16, 26.

Borghesi Niccolò, 76, 77.
Bossoli, 19 n.
Bottini, 27.
Bragadino Marcantonio : see *Marcantonio Bragadino.*
Breve dell' arte de' pittori senesi, 42, 52.
Buonconvento, 91.

CALENDAR, Reform of the: see *Reform of the Calendar.*
Calixtus III., 68, 69, 70.
Camarlingo del Comune: see *Camarlingo di Biccherna.*
Camarlingo di Biccherna, 17, 18; often chosen from the
   monastic orders, 18, 19, 20; term of office of, 20;
   duties of, 24 seq.; portraits of, 32, 33, 38, 42, 61, 113.
Camarlingo di Gabella: see *Gabella, Magistracy of.*
Campana Comunis, 22 n.
Campanella, 103.
Camullia, Battle of, 82 seq.
Camullia, Porta, 79, 84.
Capocchio, 22.
Capuchin nunnery, Destruction of, 64.
Carroccio, 22.
Casella, 22.
Castaldus Comunis, 21 n.
Castellani, 27.
Cateau Cambrésis, Peace of, 93, 94, 96.
Cathedral of Siena; Pavement of, 15 n., 66; marble for, 28.
Catherine, St., 40, 70.
Catholic Revival, 55 n., 95, 97.
Cecco Angiolieri, 22.
Chancellor: see *Camarlingo.*
Charlemagne, 57 n., 79.

Charles V., 83, 86, 89, 90, 102, 103.
Charles VIII., 78-80, 82.
Charles of Anjou, 21.
Chimæras, 71.
Cistercians, 18.
Civitas Senarum Civitas Virginis, 44.
Clement VII., 83, 86, 87.
Cognac, 83.
Colle di Val d' Elsa, 72-73.
Colour, Feeling for rich, among the painters of Quattrocento, 53, 102.
Colours of the Commune, 44, 57.
Commissioners appointed to enquire into the actions of retiring magistrates, 26.
Consiglio del Popolo, 61.
Consiglio generale della campana, 16, 25, 27, 31.
Consoli di Mercanzia, 25.
Constantinople, 59, 68.
Constitutum Palatii, 23 n.
Consuls, 17.
Corona, Albergo della, 79.
Corradino, 21.
Corruption of officials 19 n.; their punishment, 26 n.
Cosimo de' Medici, 28, 94.
Crusades, 69.
Curfew, 22.
Cusanus Nicolaus: see *Nicolaus Cusanus*.
Custos Biccherne, 23 n.

DANTE Alighieri, 22, 91.
Decoration, The five Elements of, 5.

Dietisalvi, Sienese painter, 23 n., 38.

Dodici, The, 26 n., 56 n.

Domenico Beccafumi, 81.

Don Diego Hurtado de Mendoza: see *Mendozza, Don Diego di*.

Don Giovanni de Luna : see *Luna, Don Giovanni de*.

Dragut, 97.

Duccio, 40.

Duomo: see *Cathedral*.

EARTHQUAKES of 1466-1467, The, 61-64.

Entrata and *Uscita*, 31.

Episcopatus, 21 n.

Esecutori di Gabella, 30-31.

Estimo : see *Lira or Estimo*.

Eugenius IV., 66.

Eurialo, 66.

FALCONS, 21.

Famagosta, 97.

Ferrante of Naples, 71.

Fiesole, The Bishop of, 19 n.

Fire, Compensation for houses destroyed by, 23.

Francesco I. de' Medici, 99.

Francesco di Andrea, 71.

Francesco di Giorgio Martini, 54, 60, 63, 74.

Francesco Todeschini (Pius III.), 70.

Francis of Assisi, St., 40.

Fra Paolino, 81.

Frederick II., 21.

Frederick III., 78.

French domination of Tuscany, 31.

GABELLA, Magistracy of, 28-31.
Galgano, San, 39, 40, 44.
Galgano, San, Monastery of, 18, 19, 38, 39.
Gallerani, The Blessed Andrea, 35.
Games of chance, 30 n.
Gaols, 30 n.
Gente vana, 91.
Ghiraldi Antonio Lilio, 99.
Ghiraldi Luigi Lilio, 99, 100.
Gian Galeazzo, 48, 49.
Gilio, Maestro, 23 n., 38.
Giorgio di Giovanni, architect and painter, 90, 92.
Giovanni dell'Acqua, 26 n.
Giovanni di Cristofano, 72.
Giovanni di Lorenzo Cini, 85.
Giovanni di Paolo, 56, 58, 70.
Girolamo del Pacchia, 81.
Girolamo di Benvenuto, 57 n.
Government of Siena, Allegorical representations of, 44-50, 56-57.
Granada, History of the war of, 90.
Granvela, Antoine Perrenot de, 87-89.
Gregory XIII., 99, 100, 101.
Grosso, il, the plague sore, 59.
Guccio Pieri, 26 n.
Guicciardini, 49.
Guido, Maestro, 23 n.
Guidoccio Cozzarelli, 54, 56.

HENRY II., of France, 94.
Henry VI., 17.

Holy League, The, 83.
Homines de Penitentia, 25.
Honorius III., 19 n.
Humiliati, The: see *Umiliati, Frati*.

INDIAVOLATA, Bombarde called the, 73.
Inter gravissimas, The Bull, 99.

JERBA, Island of, 97.
Jerome, St. 56.
Johann Müller: see *Regiomontanus*.
John Holywood (Johannes de Sacro Bosco), 99.
Joseph, St., 39 n.
Judex foretaneus, 31.
Julian Calendar, 98.

KNIGHTS of St. John, 96, 97.

LEPANTO, Battle of, 97.
Libertas, 57.
Libreria del Duomo, 71.
Lilian Reform, 101.
Lilius Aloysius: see *Ghiraldi Luigi Lilio*.
Lion rampant, arms of the People of Siena, 57 n., 71.
Lippo Vanni, 36.
Lira or *Estimo*, 29.
Loca venerabilia et religiosa, 41.
Lombard school of art, 51.
Lorenzetti Ambrogio, 36, 45, 45 n.
Lorenzo di Pietro (Vecchietta), 70.
Lucignano, 91.
Lucrezia di Agnolo Malavolti, Madonna, 80, 102.
Luna, Don Giovanni de, 89.

MADONNA, the « Advocata Senensium », 61, 64, 65, 69.
Madonna de' Donzelli, 36.
Madonna della Quercia in Viterbo, 63.
Madonna del Voto, 64,
Mahommedans : see *Turks*.
Malavolti Agnolo, 80.
Malta, 97.
Mangia, Letter of the, to Riccio the painter, 89.
Mantle presented by Corradino to our Lady of Grace, 21.
Marcantonio Bragadino, 97.
Markets, 30.
Martino, San, Picture in the Church of, 84, 85.
Martino, San, Terzo di, 23 n.
Mary, The Virgin : see *Madonna*.
Matteo di Giovanni, 53, 54.
Massarucio dipegnitore, 34 n.
Max Nordau's *Degeneration*, 54 n.
Medici, The 87, 94, 95.
Mendozza, Don Diego di, 89-91.
Merchant Oligarchy, 46, 46 n.
Messina, Gulf of, 96.
Meucci, a contemptuous term applied to the Sienese, 85.
Michael Angelo, 95.
Molles Senæ, 54.
Monkey of Potestà, 23.
Monopolies, Sale of, 20, 30.
Montalcino, 91, 92, 93, 94.
Montaperti, Battle of, 38, 64, 83.
Monte Amiata, 71.
Monte del Popolo, 48, 74.
Monte de' Nobili Regenti, 83.

Montefollonico, 91.

Montepulciano, 38, 78 n.

Monteriggioni, 91.

Monte Siepi, 40.

Monticchiello, 91.

Montieri, Castello di, 19 n.

Müller Johann: see *Regiomontanus*.

Mysticism, 54, 55 n.

NATIVITY, Picture of the, in the Galleria delle Belle Arti, 39 n.

Neroccio di Landi, 74.

Neroni Bartolommeo, detto il Riccio, 89.

Nicæa, Council of, 98.

Nicolas V., 67.

Nicolaus Cusanus, 99.

Nicolò da Bari, St., 56 n.

Nicolò of the Counts of Tintinnano, 23 n.

Norton, C. E., on the Cathedral pavement, 15 n.

Notary of the Camarlingo di Biccherna: see *Scrittore di Biccherna*.

Nove, The, 46, 46 n., 47, 73, 74, 75, 83.

Noveschi: see *Nove*.

OBELISK in the Piazza di San Pietro at Rome, 101.

Ochino, Fra Bernardino, 89 n.

Official corruption: see *Corruption of officials*.

Operaio del Duomo, 28.

Orgia, 21.

Ottoman Empire, 96.

Our Lady of Grace, 21.

PAGANO Pannocchieschi, 19 n.

Palazzo Pubblico, 17 n., 35, 36, 45, 67, 70, 71.

Palio, The, 28, 56 n., 85.

Paolino, Fra, 81.

Paper, when substituted for parchment in the official registers, 34.

Parentucelli Tommaso: see *Nicolas V*.

Pattern, 5, 53.

Paul II., 60.

Paul, St., 19 n., 93.

Pavement of Sienese Cathedral, 15, 66.

Pazzi Conspiracy, The, 71.

Pellegrino, San, Church of, 17.

Pennones pro capiendo et ponendo campo, 21 n.

People: see *Popolo*, *Popolani*, *Popolari*, &c.

Perches for falcons, 21.

Perrenot Antoine, Bishop of Arras: see *Granvela*.

Perugino, 81.

Peruzzi Baldassare: see *Baldassare Peruzzi*.

Petrucci Pandolfo, 75 seq.

Petrucci, The, 83.

Philip of Spain, 94.

Piazza del Campo, 17 n., 19; depicted in the Tavolette, 101.

Piccinino Iacomo, 70.

Piccolomini Alessandro, Bishop of Patrasso, 101.

Piccolomini Æneas Sylvius: see *Pius II*.

Pietro Leopoldo, Grand Duke of Tuscany, 17.

Pinturicchio, 71, 81.

Pitigliano, Count of, 85.

Pius II., 65, 67, 70, 71, 79 n.

Pius III., 70.

Piyála, 96.

Plague, The, 47, 58-60.

Poggio Imperiale, 72.

Popolani, 46 n., 93.

Popolari, 18.

Popolo, 46 n., 48, 57 n., 73.

Portraits of Camarlinghi, 32, 33, 38, 42, 61, 64, 113.

Potestà, Court of the, 17; sworn to hear complaints against outgoing officials, 26.

Prestanze, 20.

Prices paid for painting Tavolette, 23 n., 34 n.

Prisons, 30 n.

Pro pensione Biccherne, 18 n.

Protective legislation, 52.

Provenzano Salvani, 22, 38.

Provenzano, Santa Maria di, 102.

Provveditori: see *Quattro Provveditori*.

Pucci, Roberto, 85.

Purpura quam oblavit dominus Rex Curadus, 21 n.

Quattro Provveditori, 17; their numbers increased, 18; duties of, 24 seq.

Reformatori, The, 47, 73.

Reform of the Calendar, 97-101.

Regiomontanus, 99.

Religion in the Middle Ages, 40-44.

Renaissance, 51, 54, 55.

Respublica, 50.

Rhodes, The Island of, 96.

Ribaldi, 22 n.
Riccio : see *Neroni Bartolommeo*.
Ricci, Ser Iacomo di Domenico, 26 n.
Roberto Pucci, 85.
Roberto Sanseverino, Count, 80.
Rope used as emblem of civic concord, 45, 74.
Roveria pro domino Imperatore, 21 n.

SALA della Pace, 45.
Sala del Mappamondo, 71.
San Cristoforo, Church of, 22 n.
San Martino, 84, 85.
Sano di Pietro, 35, 54, 56, 70, 80, 102.
San Pellegrino, 17.
San Quirico, 91.
Sansedoni, The Blessed Ambrogio, 35.
Saviozzo da Siena, 49, 50 n.
Scipione di Crescenzio Turamini, Camarlingo di Biccherna, 99.
Scrittore di Biccherna, 24, 38.
Scrittore di Gabella, 36.
Selim I., 96.
Sena Vetus Civitas Virginis, 61 n.
Sensuality intimately connected with mysticism, 54, 55 n.
Sfondrato Francesco, 87-89.
She-wolf suckling Twins: see *Wolf*.
Siege of Siena, 93.
Sigismund, 65-67.
Significance of form, 5, 53.
Signorelli, 81.
Simone Martini, 54 n.

Sirleto, cardinal Guglielmo, 100.

Sixtus IV., 71.

Sixtus V., 101.

Sodoma, 51, 81.

Σοφία του Θεού, 56.

Space-composition, 5.

Spanish fortress, Destruction of the, 90.

Spanish hegemony, its effect upon Italian dress and
    Italian art, 102-104.

Stanchi pro ponendis falconibus, 21 n.

Stefano, Don, Camarlingo del Comune, 39.

Storia di due Amanti, 66.

St. Peter's at Rome, 101.

Suleymán I., 96.

Sumptuousness, Sense of, in the works of Matteo di
    Giovanni and Benvenuto di Giovanni, 53.

Symonds, J. A., Mr., quoted, 42, 45 n., 98, 103-104.

TACTILE values, 45 n.

Tavole, Game of, 30.

Tavole, Tavolette, 32, 35.

Tavolette dipinte, defined, 15, 16; Professor Paoli on
    the, 6, 7; Prices paid for 23 n., 34 n.; Evolution of
    the, 31-35, 55, 95-96; Effect of Spanish predomi-
    nance on the, 102-104.

Taxation, 20, 28, 29, 52.

Technique of the early Sienese Painters, 54, 54 n.

Teofilo Marzio, Cassinese monk, 101.

Terziari, 25.

Terzo di San Martino, 23 n.

Terzo, One Esecutore selected from each, 31.

Tintinnano, Rocca di, 23 n.
Tolomei Deo, 22.
Tommasi Girolamo, Camarlingo di Biccherna, 88.
Torghud, 96.
Tripoli, 96.
Turks, 68, 92, 96, 97.

Ugo da Battifolle, Count, 39.
Ugo, Don, 38.
Umbrian school of art, 51.
Umiliati, Frati, 18.
Uscita: see *Entrata and Uscita.*

Val di Chiana, 91.
Valetta, 97.
Vanni Lippo, 36.
Vecchietta: see *Lorenzo di Pietro.*
Venice, League of, 97.
Ventura, 21.
Vesillum Terzerii Sancti Martini, 23 n.
Vienna, 96.
Virgin Mary, The: see *Madonna.*
Visconti, 47.
Viterbo, 63.
Volterra, 19 n.

Wolf, emblem of Siena, 44, 57 n.

Zara, 30, 58.
Zendadarius, 21 n.

1417655R0

Printed in Great Britain by
Amazon.co.uk, Ltd.,
Marston Gate.